THe BreakIng Bad CookBook

THe BreakIng Bad CookBook

COMPLETELY UNAUTHORISED

Chris Mitchell

Photography by Jack Holmes

JOHN BLAKE

Published by John Blake Publishing Ltd,
3 Bramber Court, 2 Bramber Road,
London W14 9PB, England

www.johnblakepublishing.co.uk

www.facebook.com/johnblakebooks ⬜
twitter.com/jblakebooks ⬜

First published in hardback in 2014

ISBN: 978-1-78418-025-6

British Library Cataloguing-in-Publication Data:
a catalogue record for this book is available from the British Library.

Design by www.envydesign.co.uk

Printed and bound in Italy by L.E.G.O. S.p.A

5 7 9 10 8 6 4

Papers used by John Blake Publishing are natural, recyclable products made from
wood grown in sustainable forests. The manufacturing processes conform to the
environmental regulations of the country of origin.

contents

part 3 – dinner

part 4 – snacks

part 5 – dessert

part 6 – drinks

To my other favourite W. W.
It's an honour working with you.
Fondly,
C. M.

acknowledgements

I would like to thank all of those people who have attempted to teach me how to cook over the years, not least my mum, who wisely gave up very early on.

Francesca Ballentyne, Jamie Faber and Oliver Wiseman also need to be thanked for letting me share a kitchen with them and running the considerable risk of poisoning – or worse.

Emily Sargent, Farlie Reynolds, Emma Carter, Anna Ohrling and James Goadsby have been extraordinarily helpful when the going got too tough for me.

Toby Buchan, my wonderful editor who has whipped this book into better shape than I ever could.

And finally Jack Holmes, whose friendship and artistic prowess have been integral in making this book what it is.

introduction

If you've bought this cookbook hoping that it will be as good as *Breaking Bad* was, you're going to be disappointed. *Breaking Bad* was one of the greatest shows of all time, if not the greatest. This cookbook is probably not. So lower your expectations now. And, if you haven't bought this cookbook, then I resent you, and I don't care what your expectations are.

This book is a tribute to the two best cooks in the United States of America – and possibly the world – Walter White and Jesse Pinkman. For five seasons and sixty-two episodes they made batch after batch of the purest crystal imaginable and in the process won the hearts of everyone who watched them. Or at least Jesse did... the jury is still out on Walter. And in this book I hope I have recreated some of their greatest cooks and provided you with the recipes to do the same. From Gus Fring's exotic paila marina to Hank's quality Schraderbräu, from the famed White family breakfast to Venezia's pepperoni pizza, I try to show you the way to emulate the show's finest culinary creations.

Unfortunately, unlike Walter, I have very limited scientific expertise and, unlike Jesse, nobody to show me the ropes. What's more, I really can't cook. So for me to write a cookbook is a very questionable decision. Nonetheless, without new episodes of *Breaking Bad* to look forward to, I had been driven to increasingly desperate lengths to get my next hit, and so *The Breaking Bad Cookbook* was born. I hope that for those *Breaking Baddicts* out there going through withdrawal like I was, this book will give you the delicious relief that you need. What's more, because I'm such a rubbish cook, these recipes are remarkably easy. I can guarantee you that even if your idea of something a bit special is just to add a dash of Chili P to everything, you will still be able to pull off each and every one of these dishes. If I can cook them, anyone can.

If you haven't yet completed your journey through *Breaking Bad* and you're concerned that I'm going to give the game away, then you needn't worry. This book contains no major spoilers – although it does hint at storylines and gives away minor plot points. My remedy for this would be WATCH THE SHOW. I have no sympathy, or indeed respect, for you until you do.

All I have left to say is I hope you enjoy the book, and stay safe – whatever Walter White might try to claim, salmonella is the *real* danger.

PUBLISHER'S NOTE:
In the course of his researches for this book, the author managed to give himself a mild dose of food-poisoning. Go figure.

DISCLAIMER
The recipes found in this book are provided as suggestions only. The author and publishers cannot guarantee that favourable results will be obtained from their use, and therefore recommend that readers conduct appropriate tests under their own operating conditions. The recipes are intended for use by persons having appropriate technical skill, at their own discretion and risk. The author and publishers assume no obligation or liability, and make no warranties, with respect to these recipes.

Although every reasonable care has been taken in the preparation of the recipes and lists of ingredients in this book, the author and the publishers cannot be held responsible for any domestic accidents, fires or food poisoning, or any other accidental effects that may result from preparation of the recipes or eating of the resultant dishes.

breakfast

Without a doubt, breakfast is the most important meal of the day, and *Breaking Bad* knows this. Whether you're enforcing drug laws, teaching high school or you just have an easy day planned cooking up a fresh batch of meth, it's important to keep your body nourished with high-energy foods to keep you going all day long. *Breaking Bad* provides a number of recipes to help with this.

'I think your first big birthday decision is breakfast or lunch.'
'Um, pancakes?'

WALTER JR ANSWERS THE EASIEST
QUESTION IN THE WORLD

the traditional white breakfast

The White household is known for one thing: cooking a damn fine breakfast, and we are frequently treated to the spectacle of their morning culinary delights. Walter Jr, the true breakfast connoisseur, is rarely seen anywhere other than at the table, and there are rumours that it was written into his contract that he must be eating breakfast for 64% of his time onscreen. I can neither confirm nor deny these reports.

The breakfast combinations to be created are endless, but here's what you need to know to create the perfect White breakfast:

SERVES 3

10 large eggs
9 rashers of bacon
150 ml milk
1 large knob of butter
150 g plain flour
2 tbsp caster sugar
3 tbsp cream
1 tsp baking powder
Salt
Pepper
Maple syrup

Sift the flour, caster sugar, baking powder and ½ tsp of salt into a bowl. Then whisk 1 egg, 150 ml of milk, and 30 ml of melted butter together in a separate bowl. Pour them together and beat them until you obtain a smooth batter without any lumps. Leave to stand for a few minutes.

While waiting for the batter, heat three frying pans, one to a low heat, one to a medium heat, and one to a high heat. Break the remaining 9 eggs into a bowl and beat them thoroughly until they are evenly yellow. Add the cream and whisk it into the mixture. Then, simultaneously:

1) Place a knob of butter in the medium-hot frying pan and wait until it's melted. Add a ladle of batter and wait for it to begin bubbling. Turn it over and then cook until golden brown. Repeat until all the batter is used up. Pour maple syrup generously on the finished product.

2) Add the rashers of bacon to the hottest pan and cook for 2–4 minutes on each side, depending on how crispy you like it.

3) Melt the remaining butter in the final frying pan. Pour the eggs in and, ensuring the heat remains low, leave to cook, making sure that you stir thoroughly pretty much constantly. As the eggs thicken in consistency, stir in salt and pepper to season.

If you manage to time everything right (and I'm not your babysitter – you can work that bit out for yourself) then everything should be ready and piping hot at the same time. Serve up with salt, pepper and of course maple syrup. To fully capture the White experience, there should be a complete selection of orange juice, grapefruit juice and coffee available. If you're British, I would recommend you have tea as an option as well.

Of course, variety is the spice of life, and you will want to keep your morning routine fresh. The Whites recommend each of the following as perfectly acceptable additions or substitutions for the White breakfast:

Fruit salad, pain au chocolat, croissants, cereal, buttered toast.

the white birthday breakfast special

In a subtle link between the first episode and the first episode of the last series (perhaps they wanted to let us know how much time had passed? Perhaps there were deeper connotations? Who can really say what lies behind the mind of the show's creators?), *Breaking Bad* lets us into a little White family tradition – The White Birthday Breakfast Special.

Serves: 3

Ingredients: Exactly the same as The Traditional White Breakfast, but with extra rashers of bacon. The cook's discretion is advised on how many, depending on how much you like the birthday boy/girl. If, for example, you secretly hate your husband and don't want to be in the same house as him, let alone the same room, this is a perfect way to show how you really feel.

Exactly the same as The Traditional White Breakfast – with one key change. When serving the meal, you must cut the crispy bacon up into artistically useful pieces, before tastefully arranging the tasty morsels into the figures that represent the age of the birthday boy/girl. Only do this on their plate. Serve the others as normal.

Not only is it an aesthetically pleasing arrangement, but it also saves a bundle of cheddar on candles.

the 'if i can't kill you, you'll sure as shit wish you were dead'

Although not cooked at the White's household, this has all the hallmarks of a typical White family breakfast. Consisting of pancakes, bacon and sausages, all drizzled liberally with maple syrup, this breakfast at the local Denny's, which appears in the first episode of the fourth season, is one of the most memorable.

Having cheated death once again, and left a couple of dead bodies in their wake, the cooks are debriefing. Jesse is cheerfully tucking in with gusto while Walter White himself refuses any food, preferring to sip at a coffee instead. It becomes apparent, though, that Jesse's cheer is fairly superficial as he explains what Gus Fring is thinking: 'If I can't kill you, you'll sure as shit wish you were dead.' Perhaps not the jolliest frame of mind to be enjoying a cooked breakfast in, but needs must.

SERVES 3

The same as The Traditional White Breakfast (replace the eggs with 6 sausages)

Again, the method for this masterpiece of a breakfast is very similar to The Traditional White Breakfast's. The only difference is that you replace the scrambled eggs section with the following:

Heat a pan with a high heat and, when hot, place the sausages on it. Leave for 8 minutes, turning the sausages every 2 minutes to ensure an even cook.

To save on the washing-up (which is absolutely key, and probably the most important consideration when beginning any cook), you may wish to use the same pan for both sausages and bacon. It will have to be a big pan, but if you're a serious cook, you need the right instruments, no matter how difficult they are to source.

Perhaps try your local high school and see what you can borrow (not steal. I'm definitely not condoning stealing. OK?).

'this is your brain on drugs'

Jesse is the more unconventional of our two heroic cooks, and some of that unconventionality shines through in his wonderful take on Huevos Rancheros, the classic Mexican breakfast dish. While cooking this up as a romantic breakfast-in-bed treat for his girlfriend Jane, Jesse makes the remark that gives this recipe its name. And if anyone should know what a brain on drugs looks like, then Jesse Pinkman should.

If you want to impress your partner with your morning culinary skills, here's everything you need to know.

SERVES 2

250 ml salsa
500 g refried beans
4 eggs
8 small tortillas
125 g cheese
30 g onions
Butter
Chili P

*For those with more time — or, as I like to call it, no life — the oven can be used instead of the microwave to warm up both the tortillas and the beans. Warming food up isn't rocket science. Work it out for yourself.

First, grate the cheese and chop the onions fine, and then begin to gently heat the salsa in a saucepan.

Melt the butter in a frying pan on a medium to low heat and then crack the eggs into the pan to fry. The eggs will take around 2 minutes to cook the whites to a firm consistency while keeping the yolk wonderfully runny.

Put the tortillas in the microwave for 30 seconds on high power to warm them up. To avoid the devastating problem of two tortillas sticking together and tearing, place a sheet of kitchen roll between each one. Put the tortillas on two plates and place the eggs on top of them. Put the refried beans in the microwave and warm for between 1 and 2 minutes on high power, depending on preference.*

While the beans are warming, spoon the salsa on to the tortillas and spread to cover the eggs. Also, sprinkle the onions and half of the cheese on top.

Once the beans have reached the favoured temperature, spoon them on to the top and swirl in with the salsa, cheese, onions and egg for the 'brain on drugs' look.

Finally, sprinkle the remaining cheese on top and add a dash of Chili P for some of Jesse's signature kick. Feel free to add any other herbs or spices (oregano is a favourite) for flavour at this point as well.

Jesse's Top Tip: When cracking the eggs, ensure you leave in at least a small amount of eggshell. Not only does it add a bit of crunch and flavour, but the ladies love it too.

breakfast at hospital

While Hank is having a mid-season rest in hospital and lazing in bed all episode (i.e. living the dream), *Breaking Bad* showcases another sumptuous breakfast in the hospital café. While Walt Jr opts for his all-time favourite – pancakes – and Walt Sr goes for the sedate option of cereal, all eyes are on Marie as she struggles to deal with a potential future of being bossed around (even more...) by a rude (even more...), terse (even more...), crippled (he wasn't crippled before) ASAC Schrader. And she rises to the occasion magnificently.

SERVES 3

7 eggs
3 English muffins
500 g minced pork
½ an onion
1 ½ tsp salt
1 tsp ground black pepper
1 tsp thyme
1 tsp fennel
1 tsp oregano
½ tsp chopped parsley
Worcestershire sauce
Vinegar
Oil
Butter

Put the minced pork in a bowl and add 1 egg, the salt, pepper, thyme, parsley, fennel, oregano, Worcestershire sauce and ½ onion. Wash your hands thoroughly and then get your hands dirty by giving it a good mix until it is well combined.

Divide the meat into six equal pieces and shape them into small discs. Put a frying pan on to medium to high heat and pour some oil on. At this point, start boiling the kettle (if you have a slow kettle, you may need to do this earlier. Stop making a fool out of yourself and buy a new kettle). Take the kettle off just before it boils and pour the water into a saucepan on a hob. Meanwhile, when the frying pan is hot, place the patties on to the pan and begin to fry them. It should take about 4 minutes to cook one side, then flip and cook the other.

While the patties are cooking, crack 2 eggs into 2 cups and pour gently from a very low height into the hot water, to help keep the egg white together upon entry. Make sure the whites are separate from each other and then cover, leaving for 3–4 minutes. Once they are done, remove carefully from the water using a slotted spoon and then add the next 2. Repeat until all 6 are done.

Note: normally I would recommend store-bought English muffins. However, because I'm English I'll provide a recipe below. It takes 2 hours though! Not worth it.

Note: Adding vinegar to the water makes keeping the whites together — and separate from the other eggs — easier. It may even allow an experienced poacher to do 3 eggs at once, but I can't guarantee it. If you try that, then you do it at your own risk. What's more, the vinegar can cause the eggs to become discoloured and alter the taste slightly.

As you are plating the eggs and patties up, pop the English muffins in the toaster and lightly toast them. Butter and serve. The fantastic thing about this meal is it can be served either as a muffin sandwich or as 3 individual items. It's completely your choice.

english muffins

Here is the promised English muffin recipe. As I said before, I truly wouldn't recommend you make this. There are a lot better things you could do with two hours: watch a movie, read (some of) a book, play a whole game of football, or watch one twenty-fifth of the entirety of *Breaking Bad*. But, if you absolutely insist...

SERVES: 6 (2 muffins each)

500 g plain flour
225 ml milk
100 ml water
3 tsp butter
2 tsp active dry yeast
1 tsp sugar
1 tsp salt

Warm the milk and water in a small saucepan until it begins to bubble. Turn the heat off and then stir in the sugar until it has dissolved. Let it cool until lukewarm and then add the yeast, stirring it lightly, before leaving it in a warm place for around 15 minutes.

Sift the flour into a mixing bowl and add the salt before pouring in the yeast mixture. Mix all of the ingredients well until they have formed a soft dough that isn't too sticky. Lightly flour a surface and knead the dough on it for about 10 minutes. Put the dough back into the bowl and cover. Leave it for around an hour and it should rise to about double its size.

Uncover it and add the butter, punching the dough back down in the process. Take the dough back out and roll it out once again on the floured surface so that it's about ½ inch thick.

Lightly flour the dough and cut it into rounds with a biscuit cutter (if you don't have a biscuit cutter, my suggestion is to use your ingenuity. I find a pint glass works well) and then leave on a pre-greased baking sheet for 30 minutes, again covered, to rise. Pre-heat the oven to 180°C.

Lightly flour the top of the dough again and place the muffins on a tray in the pre-heated oven for roughly twelve minutes.

Leave to cool and then slice in two and butter. If you prefer, you can lightly toast at this point as well. Take a bite and then ask yourself, 'Was it worth it?'

walter white

Walter is *Breaking Bad*. He was there at the beginning and he was there at the end. But he sure changed a little in the middle… Whether you loved him (and we all did) or you hated him (and we all did), it's impossible to imagine a world without Walt.

An intellectual genius, Walter felt life owed him more. Which, to be fair, it did – as a co-founding member of Gray Matter Technologies, a billion dollar company, he would have hoped to have made a little more than $5,000 for his efforts. Unfortunately, he didn't, and he ended up teaching chemistry and stewing in a heap of self-pity and regret, which only multiplied when he was diagnosed with lung cancer.

Falling almost accidentally into the crystal-meth business, Walt turns his enormous intellect to making enough money to support his family through his illness and beyond. And when his alter-ego Heisenberg takes over, there's no looking back. Leaving a trail of bodies in his wake, Walter claws his way to the top of the ladder, before falling right back down again.

NICKNAME: Heisenberg; Mr White
OCCUPATION: High school chemistry teacher; car wash owner; drug lord
FAVOURITE FOOD: The Heisenburger

BEST QUOTES:
Walt to Skyler: 'Who are you talking to right now? Who is it you think you see? Do you know how much I make a year? I mean, even if I told you, you wouldn't believe it. Do you know what would happen if I suddenly decided to stop going into work? A business big enough that it could be listed on the NASDAQ goes belly up. Disappears! It ceases to exist without me. No, you clearly don't know who you're talking to, so let me clue you in. I am not in danger, Skyler. I am the danger! A guy opens his door and gets shot and you think that of me? No. I am the one who knocks!'
Walt: 'I'm the cook. I'm the man who killed Gus Fring.'
Declan: 'Bullshit. The cartel got Fring.'
Walt: 'Are you sure? That's right… now, say my name.'
Declan: 'You're Heisenberg.'
Walt: 'You're goddamn right.'
Hank: 'I don't even know who I'm talking to right now.'
Walter: 'If that's true, if you don't know who I am, then maybe your best course would be to tread lightly.'

Walt: 'It's over. We're safe.'
Skyler: 'Was this you? What happened?'
Walt: 'I won.'

mexican christmas omelettes

In a shock twist, *Breaking Bad* addicts (*Breaking Baddicts*) were left devastated and confused in Season 2 Episode 4 when Walter Jr turns down breakfast.

Walter White slaves over a stove to make some Mexican Christmas Omelettes, but his son shows his disdain for his breakfast choice (and perhaps for him) by brushing past him and out of the house. Even though his offering was spurned, any true *Breaking Baddict* – or indeed any true fan of delicious egg-based breakfasts – would want to know just what Walt was cooking up in his kitchen:

SERVES: 1 hungry, lonely person

4 eggs
50 g cheese
50 g avocado
50 g red pepper
50 g green pepper
30 ml sour cream
¼ tsp pepper
15 g onion
¼ tsp salt
Butter
Salsa
Chili P
Butter

Grate the cheese and chop the pepper, onion and avocado into small, bite-size pieces.

In a mixing bowl, mix the avocado, red and green peppers, sour cream, onion, pepper and salt, with a dash of Chili P to give it that Mexican kick which is loved by all on both sides of the Mexican border.

Melt the butter on a medium-high heat in a pan, ideally one not too big (or too small, obviously) as size matters in an omelette creation. As it does in most walks of life. While the butter is melting, whisk the eggs in a separate bowl.

Pour eggs into pan and they should immediately begin to set along the edges.

As they set, push the cooked edges into the centre, allowing the unset egg to spill over to the edges. Continue process until it is all fairly well evenly set.

Take the previously prepared mixture and spoon on to one half of the omelette, then fold it over to enclose the filling. Sprinkle the grated cheese on.

Take out of the pan and place on a plate to cool for around 1 minute. You will note that at this point the green outweighs the red in this meal in a 2:1 ratio. To redress this, spoon salsa liberally over the omelette as preference dictates.

Season with salt and pepper to taste.

For Walter Jr, this recipe was just one step too far. If you can master it (as well as all of the others, obviously) then you may well take his crown as the *Breaking Bad Breakfast Champion*. Good luck.

walter white jr

Walt Jr is a youthful high school student born with cerebral palsy who is popular, outgoing and sure loves breakfast. Because of his youth and lack of ambition when it comes to the drug trade, he's pretty much the only character to not get what's going on most of the time. A classic exchange goes something like this:

Hank (on why he has to be under police protection after pursuing Gus Fring): 'Someone doesn't like the way I've been spending my free time.'

Walt Jr. 'What, minerals?'

He is, though, one of the few unambiguously 'good' guys – just a teenager who gets caught between two warring parents and wants the family back together again. He is especially close to his father and Uncle Hank at the beginning of *Breaking Bad* but, despite his fantastic campaign to raise money through the website www.savewalterwhite.com, he becomes more and more distant from his father as time goes on. Most likely because his father is constantly lying to him, and he knows it, but very possibly just because his father stopped making breakfast for him.

NICKNAME: Flynn
OCCUPATION: High school student
FAVOURITE FOOD: Pancakes – and any other breakfast food
BEST QUOTES:
Walter Jr to Walter Sr: 'The bad way to remember you would be the way you've been this whole last year. At least last night you were... real.'
Walter Jr: 'Absolutely. Ask anyone, anybody. He's a great father, a great teacher. He knows like everything there is to know about chemistry. He's patient with you, he's always there for you. He's just decent. And he always does the right thing and that's how he teaches me to be.'
TV interviewer: 'Would you say he's your hero?'
Walter Jr: 'Oh yeah, yes ma'am, totally. My dad is my hero.'
Walter Jr to Walter Sr: 'Then why don't you just fucking die already? Just give up and die.'

'How's it taste? Bad, huh?' –
JESSE PINKMAN

lunch

Breaking Bad cares little for lunch. We are sometimes allowed access to a shot of lunch preparation, but it is a rare occasion when the *Breaking Baddict* is privy to the actual act of eating. Why that is, nobody knows. One can only imagine that, as very little actual cooking goes into a respectable lunch, our esteemed New Mexicans find the meal to be beneath them. Or maybe the film crew just refuses to work under the hot midday sun. Either way, little attention is paid to this pivotal meal.

Nevertheless, the human body needs to refuel and *Breaking Bad* provides some great simple recipes to do this.

the work lunch

Nobody prepares for a hard day's graft cooking at the lab quite as well as Walter White does. During Seasons 3 and 4, we are repeatedly treated to Walt's cultured approach to a work lunch and each meal is as meticulously and lovingly created as the last – which isn't too hard, because Walt is a creature of habit and plumps for the exact same thing every day.

But it is surely Season 3 Episode 6 that lives longest in a *Breaking Baddict's* memory, as the excitement of Walter's first day at his new job really shines through:

SERVES 1

2 slices of wholemeal bread
Peanut butter
Jam (ideally strawberry)
1 brown paper bag
1 black marker pen
1 oversized knife
NO BUTTER

Note: This is a PB&J sandwich. Peanut butter and jam. NOT peanut butter, butter and jam. For those philistines out there who insist on spreading butter on as well: I don't hate you for your sandwich-making techniques. I hate you for who you are and everything you represent.

Take 2 slices of wholemeal bread (surprisingly, Walter *White* prefers *wholemeal*... go figure) and spread peanut butter thickly and evenly on one, so that it is about ½ cm thick throughout, and jam on the other. Top tip: if you make the jam thicker in the middle and thinner around the outside, when you squash the 2 slices of bread together, the jam will spread evenly and won't leak out of the sides. You're welcome.

Squash the 2 slices of bread together and pick up the oversized knife. This should ideally be at least twice as long as the sandwich and the blade should look lethal. If it doesn't, you will have to go to a store and purchase a new one.

Position the knife just inside the crust and slice firmly to remove it. Repeat for each side of the sandwich until no crust remains.

Open the brown paper bag and place the sandwich carefully inside, ensuring none of the delicious filling spills out of the now crustless bread.

Take the black marker pen and carefully and clearly write your name on the outside of the bag. Some people might think this is ridiculous, especially if, for example, you only have one other co-worker in whichever lab you work at. But Walt knows best.

the afternoon delight

Technically, this recipe relies on other recipes. In fact, it's not 'technically'. It relies exclusively on other recipes. This isn't even a recipe. It has no place in a cookbook. Nevertheless, it's here, and it is apparently the ultimate aphrodisiac, because when Walter returns home to find Skyler in a dressing gown with green gloop on her face, as soon as she offers to make him some lunch, he can't resist some 'afternoon delight'.

Warning: this should only be made if you are both in the mood. Skyler made the mistake of misjudging her own frame of mind and things got very uncomfortable. Make this at your own peril.

SERVES 2

Leftovers (ideally something chicken-based)
1 microwave
1 fridge
1 man
1 woman

Note: Although the traditional recipe calls for one man and one woman, *Breaking Bad* is a progressive programme and embraces actions which a conservative society might disapprove of. Feel free to experiment.

Remove the leftovers from the fridge and display to your partner on the counter. Offer it to them. Put it on a plate for them, so that they know it's theirs for the taking.

Pop the plate in the microwave and watch it together as it gyrates in an alluring manner – while things begin to heat up.

When you hear a 'ding', everything should be ready. Make sure you don't leave it too long or you will find it begins to dry out. You want to maintain a moist texture where possible. Serve and enjoy.

prison food

As will most likely happen at least once in every person's life, in Season 1 of *Breaking Bad* Walter and Jesse find themselves with a guest tied up in the basement. Their faces painted a picture, and it was easy to see just how stressed they were by the pressures of hosting. It's something you won't be able to understand until the first time you find yourself in that situation, but believe me when I tell you that when someone is relying on you to provide for all of their basic bodily functions and knows that you are deciding whether they should live or die, you feel a very keen obligation to make sure that they are having a great time:

SERVES 1

2 slices of white bread
2 slices of ham
2 slices of cheese

Place the 2 slices of bread next to each other on a surface. Put the 2 slices of ham on one slice of bread and the 2 slices of cheese on the other slice of bread before closing them up to form one complete, albeit dry, sandwich.

If you are feeling adventurous, the option is there to put 1 slice of ham and 1 slice of cheese on each slice of bread. It will taste exactly the same though.

Even though they are your prisoner, they are not animals (except for in the technical sense, in which case we are all animals). Give them the option of having the crusts on or off. If they request a crustless sandwich, follow the steps as described in The Work Lunch.

Serve the sandwich on a plastic plate that cannot be shattered. There's no point in taking any risks.

Best served with: a big jug of water, ideally at least 4 litres, to make sure they get through the day without dehydrating. And some toilet roll and a bucket. Because all of this food has to go somewhere...

saul goodman

Thank God for 'Better Call Saul'; the classy lawyer who fights 'for you, Albuquerque!' with his MA in political science from the University of American Samoa and his constant stream of humorous asides.

Saul appears in Season 2 and, with his hook-ups, helps propel Jesse and Walt into the big leagues. Despite his complete sleazeball appearance and his awful TV commercials, not to mention his horribly cheap and garish office and the ribbon he constantly wears to 'show support for' the people hurt in the plane crash, Saul proves to be a very adept 'criminal' lawyer, and gets the guys out of a serious jam on more than one occasion.

Although initially he appears to know more about the business than Jesse or Walt, the roles quickly reverse, and very soon it is Walt who is causing Saul to quake in his boots. Despite this, he is unflinchingly loyal, and humorous to the very end, often showing a bigger set of balls than you would give him credit for. And surprisingly, he is often the voice of reason (although unsurprisingly, very often he isn't). Perhaps of most importance to *Breaking Baddicts* is the news that he will be appearing in a spin-off prequel show, *Better Call Saul.*

REAL NAME: Saul McGill (he pretends to be Jewish 'for the homeboys who want a member of the tribe')
OCCUPATION: Criminal defence attorney
FAVOURITE FOOD: 'Chasing Monsters'
BEST QUOTES:
Jesse: 'Mike's okay.'
Saul: 'He's okay? He said he was going to break my legs. And don't tell me he didn't mean it, okay? 'Cause he gave me the dead mackerel eyes. He meant it.'
Saul to Skyler: 'Walter never told me how lucky he was. Clearly his taste in women is the same as his taste in lawyers: only the very best... with just the right amount of dirty.'
Saul to Walt: 'Hey, what am I if not family?'
Saul: 'Look, there's always, "You gotta real nice place here. It'd be a shame if something happened to it." That angle.'
Skyler: 'What are you talking about? Violence?'
Saul: 'Attitude adjustment.'
Saul encouraging Walter: 'I caught my second wife screwing my stepdad. OK? It's a cruel world, Walt. Grow up.'

pasta salad

Yaaawwwnnnn... Skyler, I know you're an accountant, but do you have to be this boring? Why would you choose to take this to work with you? Do you sit at your desk all morning thinking, 'Well, accountancy is boring, but at least I have that pasta salad to look forward to at lunch.'? This recipe is so dull I couldn't even be bothered to think up a name for it. And, as you know from the other recipes, I don't even invest a lot of time in thinking up the names. That's how little I care about this recipe.

Pasta Salad is the sort of dish you bring to a group picnic and you know you've only done it because it's easy to make and voluminous, so it looks like you've put in a lot of effort. But we know you haven't...everyone knows you haven't. You're even worse than the people who turn up with clearly store-bought items. At least they aren't pretending to have made an effort.

SERVES 4

250 g farfalle pasta
30ml olive oil
50 g cheese
1 clove of garlic
4 plum tomatoes
Basil leaves
Salt
Pepper

Cook pasta. Chop or grate ingredients. Mix ingredients. Put in fridge.

Note: for pasta salad fans, I'm aware that there are far more interesting pasta salads out there. And I would gladly have given a more interesting, detailed, exciting recipe. But the *Breaking Bad* pasta salad sadly isn't one of them and like the *Breaking Baddict* that I am, I have to stay true to the show.

the romantic grilled cheese

This is, without doubt, the most romantic recipe in this cookbook. Walter spent weeks and weeks returning to the restaurant that Skyler worked at every day for lunch, seducing her with his sensual grilled cheese eating. For a long time he was frustrated because she wouldn't notice him but, after a while, she saw this young man, with grease running down his chin, for the person he would eventually become – chemist, lover, cook, drug baron – and she couldn't resist.

It helped, of course, that he was so damn good at *The New York Times* crossword; a lesson in romance for any young Romeo looking to win over his Juliet.

SERVES 1

2 slices of bread
100 g cheese
Butter
Worcestershire sauce

Melt about 2 tsps of butter in a frying pan on a medium to high heat. Use more or less depending on how greasy you want it to be. In general use this equation: the greater the amount of butter, the greater the amount of romance. While waiting, cut the cheese into thin slices.

Butter the 2 slices of bread and then place the cheese on one slice of bread so it is evenly spread, and add a dash or two of Worcestershire sauce for flavour. Put the other slice of bread on top to form a sandwich and then place on the frying pan.

Cover the pan with a lid (this enables the cheese to melt more quickly) and then leave to cook for 2 minutes. Add more butter (remembering the all-important equation) and then flip the sandwich. Cook for another 2 minutes until brown and crispy on both sides and serve up.

Then crack out the latest edition of *The New York Times* and show off your intellectual capabilities. This is a foolproof plan; even Badger could pull it off.

dinner

If there's one value that *Breaking Bad* can be said to have, it's the importance of family. Everything Walt does, he does to provide for his family (well, maybe not *everything*. He has a little thing for power). The closeness of his family is shown by the number of dinners they share. But *Breaking Bad* doesn't just use dinners as cosy family time. Many of the best scenes and jaw-dropping twists (notably in Season 5) happen while everyone's around for a bite to eat. I'm not going to guarantee you that if you cook these meals your life will be as dramatic as *Breaking Bad*, but I am going to hint at it very strongly with no evidence to back me up.

the white cookout

The Whites and, to be fair, the Schraders, can throw a mean barbecue. Or cookout, as they like to call it. And they don't like to keep these as quiet affairs; Season 1 sees Walt make a devastating family announcement and in Season 5 Hank makes a devastating family discovery. Basically, if you have a secret, you shouldn't host one of these cookouts.

But whatever else you can say about them, you can't say they don't make some damn tasty food. Although they are quite unadventurous with their meat selection... *Breaking Bad* seems to have an unhealthy obsession with chicken. Don't come to the White household if you want burgers or hot dogs.

SERVES 5

15 pieces of chicken (thighs, wings, legs, breast...)
5 cobs of corn
Salad* (see page 36)
10 bread rolls
Barbecue sauce
Butter
1 small head of cabbage
1 carrot
1 green pepper
250 g mayonnaise
2 tsp vinegar
¼ tsp Worcestershire sauce

Put the corn on the cob into a pot of cold water to soak for 30 minutes.

While this is soaking, fire up the barbie. If you're using a gas barbecue, this will only take a couple of minutes. However, if you rate yourself as a barbecue master then I recommend using coals. Not only does this improve the flavour to give a real smoky quality, but it also makes you feel good about yourself as a human being. It does take significantly longer though, so allow time. You know the barbecue is hot enough to cook on when you are unable to hold your hand at the height of the grill for more than a couple of seconds.

Cover the chicken in barbecue sauce and leave to soak up the juices. Core the cabbage and shred the remainder. Cut the carrot and green pepper into very small slices.

Take the corn out of the pot and slather in butter, salt and pepper. Wrap the corn in aluminium foil and put on the grill. If you are cooking with coal, put it on the outer parts where it is slightly cooler.

Immediately, put the chicken on the hottest area of the grill. If you notice areas without barbecue sauce, brush more on. Turn both the chicken and the corn regularly to ensure an even cook. Both

*In each dinner recipe where salad is an ingredient, I expect you to make a salad. I'm not going to tell you how to do it because there are literally thousands of different ways and, at the end of the day, it's all just leaves.

Top tip: The best way to ruin a cookout is by announcing out of the blue that you have incurable cancer. Even better is to then admit that you've known for weeks — I'm looking at you, Walt. Try to avoid announcements of this nature, at least until dessert.

should take around 15 minutes. Be warned that the barbecue sauce causes more flame, and more flame, unsurprisingly, causes more burned chicken.

Top tip: Barbecuing is all about flair. Flame is good, within reason. Everyone likes a bit of burn, but too much and you've ruined it. There is no science here, it's all about feel. The best thing about this is that if you're surrounded by people who aren't regular barbecuers then you can pretend it's very difficult and requires great poise and concentration.

When the chicken and corn has around 10 minutes left, take the carrot, pepper and cabbage and mix together. In a separate bowl, mix the mayonnaise, vinegar, Worcestershire sauce, ¼ tsp salt and a pinch of pepper. Add the two mixtures together and stir until the carrot, pepper and cabbage are well mixed in and softened. In case you hadn't realised, this is coleslaw.

When the chicken and corn is done, take them off of the barbecue and unwrap the corn. Slice the bread rolls and butter if required.

Best served with: Beer. If you're as manly as Hank, drop a spirit bomb in your beer to liven up the evening.

Note: to create a really successful cookout, you need at least two cooks (just like something else...), so partner up. Although *Breaking Bad* doesn't condone gender stereotypes (oh, hang on... it really does condone gender stereotypes. The whole show is one big gender stereotype), it's usually best for a male to be in charge of the barbecue and the female to be in charge of the salad and coleslaw. If only for the sake of the male's ego.

If there are two or more men present and they are both vying for control of the barbecue, the one wearing the most amusing cooking apron wins.

tuco's tacos

These tacos look suspiciously like burritos. They also taste suspiciously like burritos. But Tuco's Burritos doesn't have quite the same ring to it, so if anyone asks they're tacos, OK?

Tuco was one of the less stable characters in *Breaking Bad* and when you're talking about a show that includes a large number of meth-heads, that's quite the achievement. So when he drives Walt and Jesse out to a remote farmhouse in the boot of his car, they probably aren't thinking they're in for a great time. But Tuco never fails to surprise! Not only does he put some great entertainment on TV and wheel his uncle Hector out for some witty repartee, he's also keen to impress with a truly delicious take on the traditional taco (burrito...).

SERVES 4

500 g beef mince
200 g salsa
200 g kidney beans
4 large flour tortillas
3 tbsp tomato purée
2 tomatoes
2 green peppers
1 large onion
1 garlic clove
75 g cheese
Lettuce
Olive oil
Sour cream
Poisoned meth (optional)

Dice the tomatoes, crush the garlic, grate the cheese and chop the peppers and onion.

Heat a large frying pan over a high heat. Tuco prefers to use a flaming grill, but in the interest of both accessibility and eyebrow safety, this recipe will stick to a frying pan. Add a dash of olive oil while warming and, when hot, add the onion and garlic until they are tender, which should be 5 minutes. Add the mince and cook, making sure you stir, until it is browned, which should be another 4 minutes.

Note: at this point add any herbs or spices you might like, for example Chili P. Tuco, however, has a simple palate and prefers to keep his food like his meth: pure. If you value your safety, you won't offer him any Chili P flavoured crystal.

Add the peppers, salsa, tomato purée, tomatoes and salt and bring the heat down to medium for around another 8 minutes. Remember to keep stirring.

Heat the tortillas in either an oven or a microwave as described in 'This Is Your Brain On Drugs'. Lay them out on 4 plates and spoon the beef mixture on to the centre of each. Add cheese, lettuce and sour cream as preferred.

Once the tacos have been folded they are ready to serve.

*Poisoned meth is just one possible addition to your burrito to give it the kick that you need to get your evening going. There's a whole range of additions you can include in Tuco's Tacos, from paprika, cumin and Chili P to refried beans and guacamole. Feel free to experiment at home with fresh ideas.

'fuck you' i'm not hungry

This is the easiest recipe to follow in this cookbook, and not just because it's best served at a restaurant – although it can be just as easily served in your own home. Walter White and Gretchen Schwartz go out together and give a classic example of just how easy and effective this meal can be. A warning though: this meal does have the effect of driving people away from each other.

SERVES 2

**2 old friends
Insults**

Sit opposite each other at a table waiting for your food. Importantly, only one person can know that this dinner is being served. If you are at home rather than at a restaurant, have something in the oven under the pretence of eating it later.

Begin insulting the other person as quickly as possible. The insults should be deep and cutting; the sorts of things that, once said, can never be taken back.

If the insulter can get the insultee to leave before the food has arrived he/she will officially be declared the winner. If they do not leave, however, the insulter has failed and has to grovel in the dirt for forgiveness.

Note: very rarely does this dinner end in anything being eaten. Only undertake this dinner if a) you are not actually hungry and, less importantly, b) you have enough friends you can afford to lose one (alternatively, you might just not like people, like Walt).

venezia's pepperoni pizzeria

Venezia's has been a long-standing friend to *Breaking Bad* and is always more than willing to send over some of its fine pizzas to feed our New Mexicans. Whether they are catering for a simple family dinner, a fix-up meet between Walter and a gang of neo-Nazis or a bunch of partying meth-heads on a 3-day binge, Venezia's Pizzeria is up to the job.

And the best thing about them is that, unlike most fast food pizzerias in America, Venezia's send their pizzas to the customer uncut. The money that they save in not slicing the pizzas is passed right on to the customers – it's the deal of the century! Thanks for tipping us off about this little bargain, Badger.

SERVES 4

Dough: 225 g flour
150 ml hot water
20 ml olive oil
1 tsp sugar
½ tsp salt
5 g active yeast
Sauce: 300 g canned tomatoes
1 onion
2 celery sticks
1 carrot
1 bay leaf
3 tbsp butter
2 tbsp flour

It's important firstly to understand that a pizza is cooked in three long and tedious parts: the dough, the sauce and the topping. So you know what you're getting yourself into before you begin cooking and you can't blame me when you get bored halfway through.

The dough: Add the yeast to the hot water (40°C temperature) and stir until it dissolves. Add the oil, salt, sugar and flour. Mix thoroughly until it forms a soft dough.

Place it on a floured surface and knead for around 10 minutes until it's pleasantly smooth and elastic. Cover and leave for 1 hour to rise.

Roll dough into a circular shape. This will be a huge pizza, but that's how Venezia's does it. Transfer to a greased pan and prick the dough with a fork multiple times. Also, build up the dough around the edges to form a crust.

Bake at 200°C in a pre-heated oven for around 12 minutes, or until lightly browned.

The sauce: Chop the onion, celery sticks and carrots. Put the tomato sauce, onion, celery sticks, carrot and bay leaf into a saucepan and bring to a boil on a high heat. Turn the heat down to low and leave to simmer for 30 minutes. Remove from heat.

¼ tsp sugar
Oregano
Basil
Topping: 175 g mozzarella
cheese
225 g pepperoni

Pour the mixture into a sieve and pass through all of liquid so that just the carrot, onion, celery and bay leaf remain behind. You have to strain this really hard to make sure you maximise the liquid produced – unless you are a fan of dry, doughy pizzas. Melt the butter in a saucepan on a medium heat and add the liquid that's just been sieved. Add the flour, sugar, oregano and basil and turn the heat down to low. Leave to simmer for another 10 minutes, stirring constantly.

Season to tastiness and then leave to cool.
The topping: Grate cheese. Slice pepperoni.
The combination: Pour cooled sauce on to the crisped dough thinly and evenly. Stop 2 inches from the edge of the dough. Sprinkle cheese on and place pepperoni decoratively on top. Bake for a further 20 minutes in the oven. Remove from oven. Leave to cool, then cut it up into slices of whatever size you desire.

DON'T: Bring the pizza around to someone else's house and then throw it on to their garage roof in a fit of rage. That's a lot of wasted effort, you will immediately regret it and, ultimately, someone will just make you get a ladder and take it down. By that time, the 5-second rule will almost certainly have passed.

Easy substitution: Replace the dough-making with: pick up phone.
Replace making the sauce with: dial pizza place.
Replace making the topping with: place order and wait.

This is by far my preferred method of making pizza and I find it usually produces better results.

brandon 'badger' mayhew and 'skinny' pete

Brandon and Pete are two of the only characters who appear in every single season of *Breaking Bad* and they often bring a bit of light relief to the show, especially during one of their many 'intellectual' conversations when they are perhaps slightly under the influence. And who remembers Badger's attempts at being a professional sign-twirler? Or Skinny Pete's unexpected rendition of Bach on the electronic keyboard?

Two of Jesse's oldest friends, these guys are on hand whenever Jesse (or Walt) needs someone to help them out – or try to start a mini drug-running empire. They are both deeply affected by the death of their friend, Combo, and they even try and get clean after attending some sessions of group therapy.

Unfortunately for them, they keep getting dragged back in to their old friend's messes, but even in the final episode they have a crucial role to play.

NICKNAMES: Badger; Skinny
OCCUPATION: Meth-dealers; sign-twirler
FAVOURITE FOOD: Venezia's Pizza
BEST QUOTES:
Jesse: 'What's the point of being an outlaw when you got responsibilities?'

Badger: 'Darth Vader had responsibilities. He was responsible for the Death Star.'
Skinny Pete: 'True that. Two of them bitches.'
Skinny Pete: 'What do you think all those sparkles and shit are? Transporters are breaking you apart right down to your molecules and bones. They're makin' a copy. That dude who comes out on the other side? He's not you. He's a colour Xerox.'
Badger: 'So you're telling me every time Kirk went into the transport he was killing himself? So over the whole series, there was, like, 147 Kirks?'
Skinny Pete: 'At least. Dude, no, why do you think McCoy never liked to beam nowhere? 'Cause he's a doctor, bitch! Look it up, it's science!'
Badger while smoking a joint: 'Because I'm on probation, yo. Gotta prove to the man I'm rehabilitated.'
Jesse: 'The game has changed, yo. This is our city, alright? All of it. The whole damn place. Our territory. We're staking our claim. Yo, we sell when we want, where we want. We're gonna be kings, understand? Well, I'm gonna be king and you guys will be, like, princes or dukes or something.'
Badger: 'I wanna be a knight.'

the heisenburger

Oh, Heisenberg… you saucy theoretical physicist. Who knows why Walter chose Werner Heisenberg to be his alias and pseudonym, although maybe it had something to do with his Uncertainty Principle. This basically means that you can know either the speed or the position of a particle but not both, because merely taking the measurement of one will affect the other. (If I understand it right, which I may well not do… I'm a cook – and not even a very good one – not a theoretical physicist.) But what this boils down to on a metaphorical level is that you can't know everything, and if you try to understand it all, your interference will change the whole ball game. Kind of like how Walter and Jesse stumble through *Breaking Bad*… am I right?

Anyway, I'm thankful for Walter's choice because it makes for a very easy pun which adds a bit of zest to this simple dish which we saw the Whites and Schraders eating in Season 3.

SERVES 4

Burger: 600 g beef mince
1 onion
1 egg
20 g mustard
1 tsp salt
1 tsp pepper
Olive oil
4 bread buns
Lettuce
200 g cheese
4 gherkins

Chop the onion finely and combine in a large bowl with the mince, egg, mustard, salt and pepper until well mixed. At this point add any other herbs and spices (Chili P) that you might like to use to flavour the burgers and stir them in as well.

Divide the mixture into 4 equal parts and shape into 4 rounded burger patties.

Peel the potatoes and chop into rounds 1cm thick and then slice further into chip shapes. I prefer thick chips but thin ones are just as tasty. If you have access to a deep-fat fryer – and, let's face it, everyone should – then simply preheat to 180ºC and fry for 3–4 minutes. If you don't have a deep-fat fryer because you're some kind of insane health freak then fill a deep saucepan $\frac{1}{3}$ full with sunflower oil. Heat on a medium heat until sizzling hot and then add three handfuls of chips. Stir while they cook for 4–5 minutes and then remove with a slotted spoon and place on a tray. Repeat until all the chips are done.

Add some olive oil to a frying pan and

2 tomatoes
Chips: 500 g potatoes
Sunflower oil

put over a high heat. When hot, place the burgers on the pan and cook each side for 3 minutes.

While the burgers are cooking, add more oil to the saucepan so it is $\frac{1}{3}$ full again. Repeat the process but only cooking the chips for 2–3 minutes this time. When they are removed they should be a delicious golden brown. Place on a baking tray to cool and add salt and pepper to tastiness.

While the chips are cooling, assemble your burger with bun, lettuce, cheese, gherkin and tomato. Split the chips into 4 portions and serve up.

Unfortunately The Heisenburger isn't for everyone and, while I can't think of anything better to tuck into for dinner, Marie would disagree. She prefers the lighter option and while everyone else was happy in Season 3 with The Heisenburger she went for... sushi.

However, I certainly won't be providing you with a recipe for sushi because basically it's raw fish and rice. How hard can it be?

the cheddar barbecue

This barbecue is incredibly difficult to get right and it's definitely not for everybody. In fact, I would advise you to think long and hard before trying a recipe this extreme. The potential for disaster is certainly present and I have to admit that I have never chargrilled my cheddar. Walter White, however, pulls it off magnificently in the opening episode of Season 3; timing is everything, and he has once again shown that he is the best cook in New Mexico.

SERVES 1

Barbecue
Petrol
Shame
Regret
$500,000 of cheddar

Top Tip: try to wear non-flammable clothing. This will mean that, if any of the cheddar either catches alight properly or misses the body of water you are aiming for, you should be able to smother the flames. This will both save the cheddar from burning too much and reduce your levels of regret to manageable levels.

Note: A potentially more tasty and less expensive substitute would be to use actual cheddar cheese.

First, take a large amount of money out and stack next to the barbecue.
Note: the cheddar barbecue is best prepared near a large body of water, such as a pool or similarly well-sized area of water.

When the barbecue has reached a high enough temperature – and your shame has reached sufficient levels to mean that The Cheddar Barbecue seems like a good idea – you should squirt some petrol right over the source of the heat. This should cause some flames which are borderline very dangerous. At this point, the barbecue is ready for the cheddar to be added.

The cheddar will begin to chargrill immediately, so the timing of the next step is of paramount importance. The Cheddar Barbecue is generally caused by an overwhelming feeling of shame which causes the cook to believe that a barbecue is the right way to spend their money. The key to The Cheddar Barbecue, however, is the timing of the moment when the shame of *whatever you have done* is outweighed by the regret of burning all of your cheddar.

Walter times this perfectly, and he is able to dump his lightly chargrilled cheddar right into the pool with minimal lasting damage. However, this is extremely difficult to achieve: it is recommended that the cheddar is only kept on for a maximum time of 10–15 seconds before you flip it into the nearby water to keep from burning it beyond repair.

As a rule, it is better for the cheddar to be underdone rather than overdone.

paila marina

Breaking Bad twice treats us to the traditional Chilean dish Paila Marina, which is basically a fancy name for fish stew. In a rare moment of insight, Gustavo Fring (who here shows off his own cooking skills) admits to loving this dish just as his mother made it – which is slightly surprising because it's difficult to imagine Fring loving anything that isn't revenge or money. And even more difficult to imagine him having a mother.

What it is easy to see is what a cultured cook he is, and his recipe requires some light jazz to be played in the background while the food is being prepared.

SERVES 2

100 g large shrimp
150 g white fish, like cod
2 lobster tails
75 g clams in their shells
75 g mussels in their shells
50 g scallops
50 g calamari
80 ml chicken stock
1 large potato
1 garlic clove
½ onion
20 ml olive oil
1½ tsp lemon juice
5 g chopped parsley
Ricin (optional)

Peel shrimp, leaving the tails on. Slice the white fish into bite-sized chunks and drizzle them with 1 tsp of lemon juice and rub a pinch of salt and pepper in. Cut each lobster tail into 4 slices. Chop the potato into bite-size pieces and chop the onion finely. Make light conversation with your guest.

Heat the olive oil in a large pot on a medium heat and then add the onion, cooking for 8 minutes. Add the garlic and cook for another 2 minutes. Add the stock and some salt, pepper, the remaining lemon juice, Chili P and ricin (optional) to taste. Bring to boil, then leave to simmer on a low heat for around 20 minutes.

On a medium heat, add the lobster and cover and simmer for 2 minutes. Remove with a slotted spoon and set aside for now. Add the mussels and clams and cover and simmer for 4 minutes, when the shells should have opened. Again, remove with a slotted spoon and set them aside. Toss any that haven't opened in the bin.

Now add the potatoes and leave to simmer, again covered, for 5 minutes. Chuck the shrimp, lobster, white fish, scallops and calamari in and leave to simmer for a further 5 minutes. Chop the parsley and garnish with it, as well as the mussels and clams.

Serve up at a candle-lit table for two.

Best served with: bread, salad, white wine, difficult and tense conversation.

the return of the prodigal son

As a recipe this is fairly simple fare – a traditional Tex-Mex dinner. However, it's the atmosphere that really makes this cook a difficult one to get spot on. Normally, you might think the return of a prodigal son would be a joyous occasion, but in this case it's tempered by the fact that the Pinkmans really don't want their son, Jesse, to return at all. They would prefer to remain a compact family of three and keep their young, clever, creative, musical, (weed smoking) son pure of any taint that Jesse might bring back with him.

So part of the secret of this recipe is to invite someone you don't like, plaster a smile on your face and leave much of what you're actually thinking unsaid, while making it clear to whoever you don't want to be there, that you really don't want them to be there. And you have to do all of this while still enjoying the food.

SERVES 4

600 g chicken breast
500 ml chicken stock
8 flour tortillas
5 garlic cloves
2 onions
1 tbsp paprika
1 tbsp oregano
1 tsp cumin
Salt
Pepper
Chili P
Olive oil

Dice the chicken breast into small, bite-size pieces. Chop the onion finely and mince the garlic cloves.

Pour olive oil into a large saucepan and heat on a medium heat. Add the onions and cook for around 8 minutes until soft, before adding the garlic and cooking for another 4 minutes.

At the same time, rub the chicken with salt and pepper and heat some olive oil in another pan on a medium to high heat. Toss the chicken in and cook until browned for around 8 minutes.

Add the paprika, oregano, cumin and Chili P to the onion pan and cook for another 2 minutes. Transfer the chicken into the same pan and pour the chicken broth in. Bring it to a boil on a high heat and then bring the heat down and leave it to simmer for around 20 minutes. Season with salt and pepper and Chili P to taste.

While that is simmering, warm the refried beans in the microwave, grate the cheese, slice the tomatoes thinly and shred the lettuce. Serve up as sides along with the sour cream, salsa and guacamole to

300 g refried beans
2 tomatoes
100 g cheese
Lettuce
Sour cream
Salsa
Guacamole
Salad

help build the perfect customised taco.

Pour the chicken into a bowl (the sauce should now be very thick) and warm the tortillas in either the microwave or oven as described in This Is Your Brain On Drugs. Serve up whatever salad you have prepared as a side as well.

Allow guests to create their own taco creations.

A great way to ensure that the prodigal son – or whichever guest is there that you don't want to be there – knows he or she is unwanted is to secretly prick their soft taco wraps so that no matter how well folded their taco is, the sauce inevitably drips out and makes their fingers messy. A truly diabolical plan.

i'm the guy

The Guy is an important role to have in _Breaking Bad_ and it is a good one to play, full of brooding silences and lethal glares. Unfortunately, events can be pretty lethal for The Guy too, leading to a string of fairly violent deaths. Nevertheless, when Jesse gets the chance to be Mike's Guy he jumps at it and everyone is happy for him, except maybe Walter White.

One of the many perks of being The Guy – apart from having the opportunity to work long hours at two jobs, and the pleasure of spending a great deal of time in the company of the ever-charming and witty Mike Ehrmantraut – is sharing meals with Mike in his favourite diner. So, if you fancy your chances of being The Guy, have a crack at this recipe:

SERVES 2

200 g lamb mince
200 g beef mince

Preheat the oven to 180ºC.

Put the mince, the egg, the garlic clove (finely minced), the tomato purée, the breadcrumbs (or oats), the mustard, the

sage, the tarragon, the marjoram, the dash of Worcestershire sauce and around 1 tsp of salt and pepper into a large loaf tin or oven dish and mix.

1 egg
1 garlic clove
2 tbsp tomato purée
75 g breadcrumbs or oats
1 ½ tsp mustard
1 tsp sage
½ tsp tarragon
½ tsp marjoram
A dash of Worcestershire sauce
Salt
Pepper
500 g potatoes
100 ml milk
2 corn on the cob

Mush it all together for around 5 minutes until all of the ingredients are thoroughly mixed in. If the mixture seems too moist, add slightly more breadcrumbs. If it's too dry, add more purée.

Once you're happy with the consistency, form the meat ball into a loaf shape, patting it to ensure there are no air bubbles remaining in the middle.

Place in the centre of the oven dish or loaf tin and put into the oven for around 45 minutes.

While the meatloaf is cooking, peel the potatoes and cut them into chunks. Put the potatoes into a saucepan and cover with water. Bring the water to a boil on a high heat and then turn the heat down to low so that it remains simmering. Cover and leave for 20 minutes.

While the potatoes are simmering (and the meatloaf is baking), shuck the corn on the cob (far easier to buy them pre-shucked) and then pop them into another saucepan filled with cold water. Put a high heat on and bring the water to a boil. Once the water has reached boiling point, the corn is cooked.

After the potatoes are done, drain the water, bring the milk to a boil (in another separate saucepan – I hope you have enough) and then pour the milk over the potatoes. Mash and mash and mash until the potatoes are smooth. This can be very therapeutic. Season with salt and pepper as desired.

Time it right, and everything will be done at once. Don't time it right, and you aren't The Guy – and you probably never will be.

mike ehrmantraut

Mike really is The Guy. Sure, he has a Guy himself, but that just goes to show how much of a Guy he is.

His role as Gus Fring's enforcer/hitman/consigliore/Guy gives great pleasure to *Breaking Baddicts*. With his slow, measured movements and his menacingly hooded eyes his character conveys the optimum amount of menace and control to make him scary while, at the same time, lovable.

As a man, he is tough but fair; he won't hesitate to kill you if you deserve it, but he doesn't like violence for violence's sake. Then again, if he hates your guts – like Walter's – then he isn't likely to forget it any time soon. Despite his great judge of character, events – and his loyalty to his many Guys – force him into a partnership he doesn't want to be in, and he ultimately pays the price for it. I hope his granddaughter gets a bit of the cash he worked so hard for.

NICKNAME: Are you kidding?
OCCUPATION: Cop in Philadelphia; private investigator; hitman; The Guy
FAVOURITE FOOD: The 'I'm The Guy'
BEST QUOTES:
Mike: 'I'd like you to exit your vehicle and start walking toward us.'

Walter: 'And then what? I'm gonna need some... some kind of assurance.'
Mike: 'I assure you I could kill you from way over here if it makes you feel any better.'
Walter: 'Just... just a warning?'
Mike: 'Hmph. Of course. Just trying to do the right thing. But two weeks later he killed her. Of course. Caved her head in with the base of a Waring blender. We got there, there was so much blood you could taste the metal. The moral of the story is, I chose a half measure when I should have gone all the way. I'll never make that mistake again. No more half measures, Walter.'
Saul: 'Attorney-client privilege. I mean, that's a big one. That's something I provide for you. I give up Pinkman, well, then you're gonna be asking, "Ol' Saul gives 'em up pretty easy. What's to keep him from giving me up?" Y'see, so, then where's the trust?'
Mike: 'I trust the hole in the desert I'd leave you in.'
Mike to Jesse before he became The Guy: 'You are not the guy. You're not capable of being the guy. I had a guy but now I don't. You are not the guy.'
Mike to Walt: 'Just because you shot Jesse James, don't make you Jesse James.'

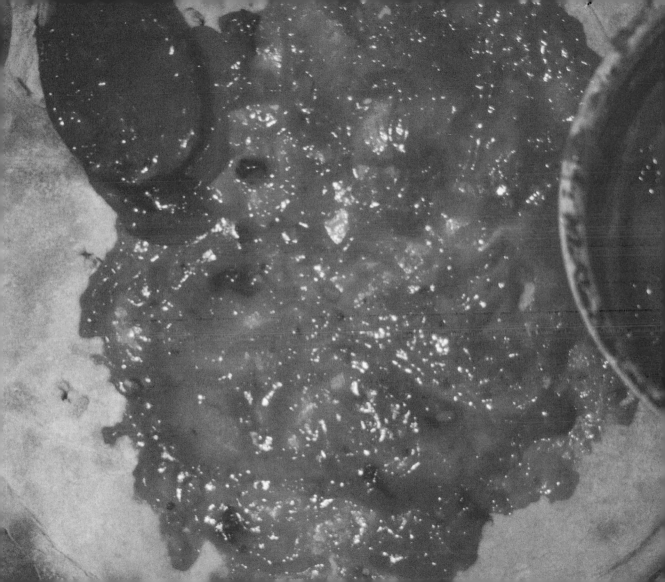

the awkward dinner

There might be a time when you've sat at the dinner table and thought to yourself, 'This is incredibly awkward. I don't think anything could be more awkward than this.' But you were wrong; it could be. And when Walt invites Jesse to stay for dinner with himself and Skyler the atmosphere is as awkward as it gets. Skyler is only interested in drinking white wine and bringing up her affair; Walter picks at his food and pretends everything is OK; while Jesse is left in the middle – like an only child in the middle of a horrible divorce – trying to make small talk and act as though nothing's wrong.

Unfortunately, Jesse's small talk involves complimenting the store-bought green beans and explaining what it's like to live off scabby ready meals from the microwave, so Walter's plan to bring Jesse into the family fold fails in a hilariously horrible manner. If you're ever planning a dinner which you know in advance will be truly awkward, this is what you need.

SERVES 3

Lamb: 6 lamb steaks
2 cloves of garlic
Olive oil
Rosemary
Salt
Pepper
Potatoes: 750 g potatoes
150 ml milk
Cornbread: 250 g cornmeal
450 ml milk
180 g flour

Mince the garlic cloves and then put the lamb steaks in a large bowl with the garlic, rosemary, and enough olive oil so that they are covered and leave to marinade for 1 hour (or longer).

Preheat the oven to 200°C and grease the tin with some butter. Add the cornmeal and the milk together and let it rest for about 5 minutes.

In a separate bowl, whisk the flour, baking powder, eggs, sugar and salt together and then add the butter and cornmeal mixture. Keep on whisking until it's quite smooth.

Pour the batter into the pan and leave it to bake for around 20–25 minutes

Prepare the potatoes for mashing by peeling and then follow the method as described in the previous recipe, I'm The Guy, for mashed potatoes. After peeling, the process should take around 25–30 minutes.

Chop the almonds into small, thin slices and trim your green beans. Heat

2 eggs
1 tbsp baking powder
1 tsp salt
9 × 13 inch tin (or similar size)
Beans: 350 g green beans
2 tbsp butter
1 ½ tbsp almonds
1 ½ tsp lemon juice
Olive oil
Salt
Pepper

a small pan and toast the almonds for 2 minutes, stirring constantly. Take them off the heat and leave them to cool.

Heat a griddle plan with a high heat and then season the lamb with salt and pepper. Put the lamb steaks on the griddle and cook for about 3 minutes on each side, depending on preference and thickness of the meat.

At the same time as the meat is cooking, pour water into a saucepan and bring it to boil. Add the green beans and a bit of salt and cook for 4 minutes. Drain the water away and throw in the almonds, butter, lemon juice and some salt and pepper. Stir it all up and when the butter is melted, serve up with potatoes, cornbread and lamb for a delicious, if fairly silent, meal.

Note: unbelievably, this isn't actually the most awkward dinner *Breaking Bad* treats us to. That occurs in Season 5 between Walt, Skyler, Hank, Marie and a waiter who is not a good judge of atmosphere. However, the dinner is actually too awkward to take place and is over before any food is ordered, so this doesn't count.

the blowfish

The blowfish doesn't exactly spring to mind when thinking of heroic animals, but Jesse was honoured when Walt told him he was one. Well, not at first – but once Walt explained his reasoning he felt a bit better about it. So, in honour of Jesse 'The Blowfish' Pinkman, I thought I would provide *Breaking Baddicts* with a top-notch traditional Japanese recipe.

But it turns out it's really easy to die from eating them – which may be because their flesh contains extremely potent toxins. And it's just fish! So, ultimately, it's just not worth the fuss.

I will leave you with the knowledge that one of the most poisonous, and allegedly tastiest, areas of the blowfish is their balls. How that fits in with the Jesse as blowfish metaphor is anyone's guess. But his girlfriends don't tend to have the greatest luck...

the 'i fucked ted' pot roast

After a long, hard day in the lab, if you come home and smell the unmistakable aroma of beef roasting in the oven, you must feel on top of the world. And Walter certainly looked it when he strolled into his house like the king in his castle. However, he came crashing right back down to earth when Skyler dropped her vengeful little bombshell: 'I fucked Ted'. Not only does Walter have to deal with being cuckolded, it's by Ted Beneke – someone who can only keep his business afloat by committing serious fraud, gets caught in the act and manages to do himself serious damage tripping on a rug. Not exactly alpha male material...

Then again, at least Walter had the pot roast to cheer him right back up, and who could fail to be cheered by that? This one takes a little while, but it's worth it. Much more worth it than English Muffins, that's for sure.

SERVES 4

1 kg beef
6 carrots
5 onions
2 celery sticks
100 g mushrooms
500 ml beef stock
115 ml olive oil
1 bay leaf
A decent handful of thyme sprigs
1 tbsp butter
3 tbsp flour

Preheat oven to 160ºC. Rub the hefty chunk of meat with about 5 ml of olive oil, salt, pepper and plenty of thyme. One important rule to follow in a roast is there's never enough thyme. Put it in a flameproof casserole dish and brown on a high heat for about 5 minutes. Ideally, you should sear each side of the meat which helps it stay moist while being roasted.

While doing this, add 10 ml of olive oil to a frying pan and on a medium heat, cook the carrots, celery and onion (all of which should be chopped, but into large pieces)

for around 8 minutes.

Pour the stock into the casserole dish and arrange the vegetables (onion, carrot, celery and mushrooms) all around the meat. Add the bay leaf and some more thyme. Cover and pop it into the oven for 1 hour and 30 minutes.

While this is cooking, peel the potatoes and cut them into roughly 4 equal pieces (you've seen how big roast potatoes are meant to be – cut them to that size). 15 minutes after putting the meat in the oven, pour the remaining 100 ml of olive oil into

Salt
Pepper
1 kg potatoes
Salad

a roasting tin and place that in the oven to heat up.

Put the potatoes in a pan and cover with water. Add a bit of salt for flavour and put a high heat on to bring the water to boil. Lower temperature to a medium heat and leave to simmer for a couple of minutes.

Drain the water and give the potatoes a vigorous shake to soften them up. Sprinkle 1tbsp of flour on to them and then place them carefully in the hot oil. Don't toss them in, because boiling hot oil splashed on the face doesn't feel that wonderful. Roll them so that they are all completely covered in the oil.

Turn the oven up to 200ºC and put the potatoes in to roast. Leave for 45 minutes,

but turn them over at 15-minute intervals to ensure a fairly even cook.

Take the roasted meat out of the oven and cover it in a tent of foil to cool for 10 minutes. While it is cooling, turn the oven up to 220ºC and leave the potatoes in to make them nice and crispy. Carve the meat, take the potatoes out of the oven and them put the beef, vegetables and potatoes on plates to serve. Sprinkle the potatoes lightly with salt and pepper.

Put the remaining liquid over a high heat and add the butter and 2 tbsp of flour. Stir in vigorously to create a jus (what posh people call gravy) to serve with the roast.

And don't forget the side salad.

skyler white

It's hard not to feel sorry for Skyler. If hardened criminals can't stand up to Walt and his mind games, what chance does she have?

The early seasons show that Skyler really does love Walt, and his cancer diagnosis hits her hard. However, as time goes by, and their relationship becomes more and more strained by Walter's repeated deceptions, she becomes increasingly isolated – something which will only become worse for her.

Although initially it appears as if Skyler is quite a weak character, pretty soon it becomes apparent that she can be every bit as tough as her husband. Whether it's getting revenge on Walt for putting her through hell ('I fucked Ted'), coming up with ingenious plans to help the criminal operation (the A1 Car Wash), or just protecting her family (sending the kids away to Hank and Marie's) Skyler has proven time and again that she is more than a match for her husband.

And Saul is just as frightened of her as he is of Walt.

NICKNAME: Sky; Mrs White
OCCUPATION: Bookkeeper; car wash manager

FAVOURITE FOOD: White wine
BEST QUOTES:
Skyler to Walt: 'Someone has to protect this family from the man who protects this family.'
Skyler: 'I need support. Me, the almost 40-year-old pregnant woman with the surprise baby on the way. And the husband with lung cancer who disappears for hours on end and I don't know where he goes and he barely even speaks to me any more. With the moody son who does the same thing. And the overdrawn checking account. And the lukewarm water heater that leaks rusty looking crap and is rotting out the floor of the utility closet and we can't even afford to fix it! But oh, I see! Now I'm supposed to go, "Hank, please, what can I possibly do to further benefit my spoiled, kleptomaniac bitch sister who somehow always manages to be the centre of attention?" Because God knows she's the one with the really important problems!'
Walt [showing Skyler a pack of cigarettes]: 'Perhaps you know something about these?'
Skyler: 'Perhaps. Then again perhaps I don't, Walt. Perhaps I smoked them in a fugue state.'
Skyler to Walt: 'I never wanted any of this.'

cooking the books

When people think of cooking, they inevitably immediately think of cooking crystal meth, and then of cooking food. However, this misses out a key component of everyday life in the business world: cooking the books. And if Walter White is the king of the lab, then Skyler White is the king of the accounts.

It may not have quite the same sexiness to it (not to take anything away from Skyler), but Skyler proves to be just as adept at scheming and manipulating as her husband when she cooks the books, first for Ted Beneke and then for the Whites themselves at their car wash.

Even when she and Ted are caught red-handed with their hands in the cookie jar, Skyler is able to dazzle the IRS with her accounts mumbo-jumbo – or lack of it – and comes out on top. So this is a tribute to Skyler White, one of New Mexico's finest.

SERVES 1

A shitload of illicit cash
1 struggling business
Invisible customers
1 knowledgeable accountant
A lack of governmental oversight

Take your cash and charge your invisible customers for equally invisible services rendered through your struggling business.

Place the cash into the cash register and write a receipt.

Have your accountant cook the books so that the money looks like it has come from real and legal customers.

Use the lack of governmental oversight to transfer your successfully laundered cash straight into your bank account.

'can i have a 'stang?'

Imagine you are asking for a big favour or gift from someone. You invite them for dinner to smooth them over and trick them into giving you what you're asking for. But what should you cook them? It could make or break the evening and your chances of getting what you want.

Well, fortunately, as ever *Breaking Bad* is able to show the way, and this meal is so effective that even though Walter Jr didn't even cook it, he still felt the time was right to ask for a Mustang for his 16th birthday. Was it effective? Well, over the two-year span of *Breaking Bad* he is bought an incredible three cars by his parents. What can this magical meal be? Unbelievably, the secret recipe is just a classic spag bol.

SERVES 3

300 g spaghetti
400 g beef mince
300 g chopped tomatoes
200 ml beef stock
100 g cheese
60 g mushrooms
1 large onion
1 clove of garlic
1 tbsp olive oil
1 tbsp tomato purée
1 tsp oregano
Chili P
Worcestershire sauce

Chop the onions then put the olive oil in a large pan over a high heat and toss the onions in for 4 minutes. Mince the garlic clove and then add both the garlic and the mince. Fry until the mince is brown.

Chop the mushrooms and add them along with oregano, Chili P and salt and pepper. Cook for 3 more minutes before adding the tomatoes, beef stock, tomato purée and Worcestershire sauce.

Bring the whole lot to boil and then reduce the heat to a low to medium heat, cover and then leave it to simmer for around 30 minutes. Stir it occasionally.

While that's cooking, bring some water to boil and chuck in the spaghetti. Pasta takes different amounts of time depending on the type you use, but you normally need to cook it for around 10 minutes. Supposedly you can check if the pasta's done by chucking it at the wall, but that wastes pasta, makes the wall greasy, and is probably bullshit anyway.

Once the pasta and meat are both cooked, put them in the same pan and stir in the sauce. Cook for a couple of minutes to allow the spaghetti to become infused with the bolognaise goodness.

Grate the parmesan and serve up, sprinkling the cheese liberally on top.

LOS POLLOS HERMANOS

That's right – I've saved the best for last. Los Pollos Hermanos. The Chicken Brothers. The one-stop shop to fast food heaven.

Los Pollos has a sterling reputation in the New Mexican community, predicated on its promise of only using the freshest herbs and ingredients, and the fact (which is in fact largely a fiction) that it's a proud family business. What's more, Gustavo Fring, the revered owner, is an outstanding member of the community, contributing his support and money not just to the police force but also to hospitals, schools and universities. What a guy.

What isn't known quite as widely is that the fry batter occasionally contains a secret ingredient which isn't exactly fresh, but is certainly chemically pure and gives the chicken a little kick. The formula for this secret ingredient is a carefully kept secret worth hundreds of millions of dollars, so I unfortunately won't be able to share the recipe with you. However, it is almost certainly what gives Los Pollos the edge over KFC in the minds of *Breaking Baddicts*.

As Los Pollos Hermanos features so heavily throughout the show, it's important that you should be able to sample some of the menu. This is most easily done with the use of a deep-fat fryer but, as most households don't seem to have one of these, the recipes provided will not make use of one. For best results though, both in terms of tastiness and healthiness, a deep-fat fryer is recommended.

a bucket of chicken

The most important thing about this classic meal is that it has to be served from a paper bucket. Scientists are split on why this is so important – some believe it is because of the way the grease interacts with the paper, others believe it's more of a psychological effect. But whatever it is, there is no doubting the end result – a great feeling of well-being.

The bucket of chicken appears on a number of occasions in *Breaking Bad*, not least as comfort food for all the family while Hank was in hospital, and it can take any of three forms: mild, medium or – Hank's favourite – *muy caliente*. This recipe should provide you with everything you need to create your own nutritious and wholesome Bucket of Chicken.

SERVES 4

1 kg chicken (any part works:
thigh, breast, wing, beak...
that's the beauty of frying it)
800 ml buttermilk
250 g flour
200 ml vegetable oil
2 cloves of garlic
1 large paper bucket
Salt
Pepper
Chili P

Rub a decent amount – just under a tbsp – of salt and pepper into the chicken. Season with Chili P as preference dictates.

Mince the garlic cloves and put them and the buttermilk into a large bowl. Drop the chicken in to tenderise it. This can be left anywhere from 15 minutes to overnight, depending on how tender you want the chicken (and how far you can be bothered to think in advance. Leaving it overnight takes the 'fast' bit out of 'fast food'). Mix the flour with salt, pepper and Chili P and remove chicken from buttermilk to roll in the flour. Coat thoroughly.

Heat the oil in a deep saucepan on a high heat until sizzling hot. (To check, you could drop a little bit of bread into it. If it gives a satisfying sizzle immediately on entry, then it's hot enough.) Add the chicken – depending on how big your saucepan is, you will almost certainly have to do this more than once, as all the chicken won't fit – and cook for 12 minutes.

It should now be a satisfying golden brown. Remove with a slotted spoon and place on a paper towel. If you need to cook more chicken, pop the first lot in the oven on a low heat to keep hot.

When all the chicken is ready, dump it all into the paper bucket and serve.

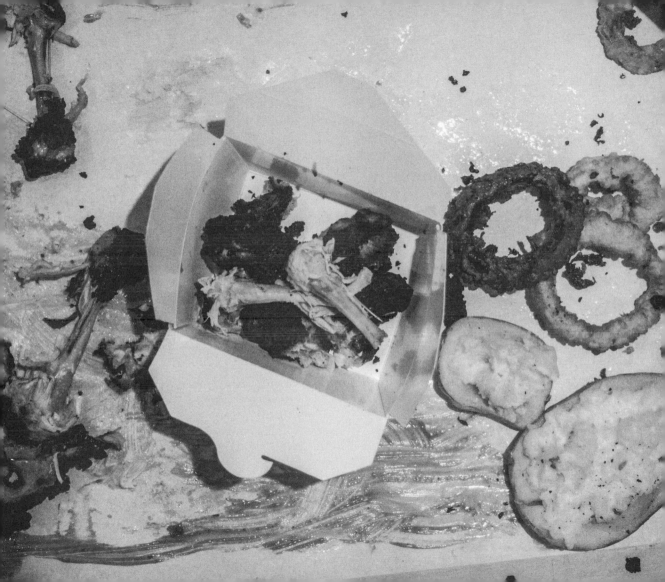

onion frings

This is Gus's favourite side; so good he's named it after himself, and there's a rumour that he demanded the director include a brief shot on camera of them going into the Los Pollos deep-fat fryer with some chicken, which there was in Season 3 Episode 6. Walter White is a big fan of them as well, and often orders an Onion Fring when he drops by Los Pollos for a quick natter with Gus or Mike.

SERVES 4

4 large onions
250 ml milk
150 g flour
1 egg
1 tsp salt
½ tsp baking powder
¼ tsp pepper
200ml vegetable oil

Skin the onions and cut them cross-wise to slices about ¼ inch long. Arrange them into ring shapes.

In a mixing bowl, mix 100g of flour, salt, pepper and baking powder together. In a separate bowl, whisk the milk and egg together and then combine the two mixtures, stirring well.

While doing this, pour the vegetable oil into a deep saucepan and heat on a high heat until sizzling hot. Dip the onion rings into the batter, then into the remaining flour, and then into the batter once more to ensure that they are covered thoroughly.

Drop the onion rings in and fry until they are a light brown, which should only take a couple of minutes.

Remove with a slotted spoon and place on a paper towel to drain the oil off.

gustavo fring

The mild-mannered Chilean model businessman with a mysterious past; little is known about Gus before he surfaces in Mexico looking to enter the meth trade. But whatever he was doing it can't have been at all good because his reputation was enough to save his life when the Mexican cartel was threatening. And if it had anything to do with Pinochet, it was probably really bad...

Fring and Walter are two very similar people who end up going down two very similar roads. They both want to build a drugs empire, but there's only room in town for one meth-king, and so the game of killer cat-and-mouse begins between Fring and his one-time protégé.

What's possibly the most frightening aspect of Fring's character is his facial expressions, which range from almost no emotion to no emotion. No other character could hold a room's complete attention for an entire 5 minutes without uttering a word or showing emotion, but when he has Jesse and Walter tied up in the laboratory, he does it.

Even when he smiles (which is very rare) he is dead behind the eyes. Chilling.

NICKNAME: The Chicken Man
OCCUPATION: Drug lord; co-founder of Los Hermanos Pollos; entrepreneur
FAVOURITE FOOD: Paila Marina

BEST QUOTES:
Gus to Walter: 'What does a man do, Walter? A man provides for his family. And he does it even when he's not appreciated, or respected, or even loved. He simply bears up and he does it. Because he's a man.'
Gus to Walter: *'If you try to interfere, this becomes a much simpler matter. I will kill your wife. I will kill your son. I will kill your infant daughter.'*
Gus offering his help to Walter: 'Well, when I first started out, I made a lot of mistakes. More than I care to admit. I wish I had someone to advise me, because this life of ours, it can overwhelm. You are a wealthy man now, and one must learn to be rich. To be poor, anyone can manage.'
Gus taunting Hector: 'This is what comes of blood for blood, Hector. Sangre por sangre.'

stuffed potato skins

If you are ever involved in – or the cause of – a police shooting, the most important thing to remember is to not let the police know you were involved. If that means poisoning anyone who survives, then so be it. The next most important point is to give them all free food so that they think you're a top bloke which, let's face it, if you have managed to literally get away with murder, you probably are.

Chips are a classic side that almost can't be improved upon, and the recipe for them can be found as a crucial part of The Heisenburger. But, if you want to try something a touch more classy – which, if you are trying to give off the impression of someone who isn't a murderer, isn't a bad thing – you could do worse than some Stuffed Potato Skins.

SERVES 4

4 large potatoes
200 g cheese
20 ml milk
3 tbsp butter
3 tbsp cream cheese
2 tbsp vegetable oil
Salt
Pepper

Bake the potatoes in the oven – preheat to 200ºC and prick the potatoes' skins so that steam can escape. Put the potatoes in and leave for 50 minutes.

Add the vegetable oil to a baking tray and put it in the now-empty oven. Turn the temperature down to 180ºC

Cut the potatoes in half lengthways and scoop out the potato pulp from the middle. Leave about 1cm around the skin though.

Add the butter, milk, cream cheese and around 1 tsp of salt and pepper to the potato pulp and mix thoroughly until it's smooth and creamy.

Keep an eye on the oil in the oven. When it's hot pop the potato skins on to the tray and roast until they are golden, which should be 5 minutes or so. Now grate the cheese.

Remove the tray and take the potato skins off. Spoon the potato mixture into the potato skins and sprinkle the grated cheese on top. Pop the skins on to the tray and put them back in the oven for another 5 minutes.

Serve up to some thrilled police officers (or anyone else you are trying to convince you are a stand-up citizen who would never be involved in murder or drug-trafficking).

snacks

You've had a tough day, cooking for hours in the 'crystal ship' and you're only halfway through the latest batch. The last thing you want to do is to worry about what there is to eat. But don't worry; *Breaking Bad* understands this, which is why it provides us with a healthy – and sometimes unhealthy – array of snacks to keep us going in almost every situation with a minimal amount of prep time.

'Wow, I feel, like, sorry for your tastebuds' –
WALT JR.

intervention snacks

Hosting an intervention can be a lot of pressure, as I'm sure you know. It combines all the stress of hosting a party with the fact that everyone knows it's going to be long and boring. For a host, making an intervention fun is as difficult as nailing jelly to a tree, or reaching 99.2% purity in your cook.

In my experience, one way of livening things up is to play a game to see how quickly you can make the guest of honour cry, and then start a pool to take bets on the result. If, however, you are hosting the intervention for a bunch of chumps who have a moral issue with gambling on someone's psychological well-being, then the food you serve is another area in which you can work to get the party going.

Skyler throws a classic intervention party in the first season for Walt, to celebrate the recent news of his cancer diagnosis and hers is certainly a good model to follow for any party you throw in the future.

SERVES 5

300 g cheese
A variety of crackers
1 bunch white grapes
1 bunch purple grapes
30 strawberries

It's very difficult to go too wrong with this recipe.

The cheese can be of one variety or many, depending on what you have in the fridge and how much of a cheese connoisseur you and your guests are. Cheddar is the classic go-to cheese, but you can experiment with all sorts, from feta and mozzarella to bocconcini and halloumi.

The crackers can again be of any variety, but it's best to go for crackers that are nice on their own – nothing too dry or plain – because your guests won't necessarily be able to take the time to build themselves a proper cheese cracker as they have to be seen to be paying attention and not just concerned with their own stomachs. Even though they will probably be bored and wishing they could just tuck in. Salty biscuits, like Ritz, are the best bet.

Give the fruit a quick wash, cut the cheese into 1-inch cubes, spread the

crackers out, pluck the grapes off the vine and remove the stems from the strawberries.

Serve up, ideally on one big platter, but if necessary on a series of small plates, and cover with clingfilm.

Important note: nobody is allowed – and I'm looking at you, Hank Schrader – to eat until the guest of honour has arrived. The clingfilm is key to keeping prying fingers off of the grub until everyone is present. This is also important because, like the ever-curious meth-head, people crave what they can't have. Time things so that the majority of your guests arrive at least half an hour before the guest of honour so that they become hungry and greedy. This has the unfortunate side effect, though, that you have to make conversation with them for a longer period of time.

Intervention Top Tip: If you've ever read *Lord of the Flies* you know how important the conch is. Well the talking pillow has the same mystical importance. It's key to the success of the party that people RESPECT the pillow and only speak while holding it.

Also, Hank – who it appears has been to this sort of rodeo before – exemplifies the best techniques to get through the evening. If you can speak only in long-winded analogies, preferably about sports, which have no obvious (or even oblique) relation to the issues at hand, then you have done your job well.

marie schrader

Skyler's sister Marie begins *Breaking Bad* as a very irritating character. Not only does she have annoying kleptomaniac tendencies, but she has a habit of being able to ask just the right questions to get under people's skin (as well as just talking a heck of a lot). She is also quite vain and is very picky about her food. And she is obsessed with the colour purple.

However, as time goes on she comes increasingly into her own and is the emotional (and at times physical) support her husband needs to get him through some tough days. More than that, though, as the series enters its final stages she shows some real anger towards those that have wronged her and her family, as well as genuine emotion, which makes you sympathise with her all the more.

Plus she has to put up with grouchy Hank every day. That would be enough to make anyone go a bit crazy.

NICKNAME: Tori Costner or Charlotte Blattner
OCCUPATION: Lab technician in the radiology department
FAVOURITE FOOD: Sushi
BEST QUOTES:
'Chemotherapy and marijuana go together like apple pie and Chevrolet.'

setting up an empire pretzels

'Jesse, you asked me if I was in the meth business or the money business. Neither. I'm in the empire business' – Walter White

Empire-building is a tricky business and it's not something I would recommend. It all has a habit of blowing up in your face – literally for one unfortunate kingpin. But if Gus Fring and Walter White couldn't make it work, the chances of Jesse Pinkman running a really successful and trouble-free criminal consortium were slim to none, I'm afraid.

Nonetheless, when he gets his boys – Badger, Combo and Skinny Pete – around for pretzels and Pepsi, hope is in the air. If you're ever considering carving out some territory of your own, you could do worse than making this to kick-start things.

SERVES 4

400 g flour
15 ml active yeast
200 ml warm water
600 ml hot water
40 g white sugar
60 g baking soda
50 g salt
2 tsp vegetable oil

Note: These are, obviously, savoury pretzels. If you have a sweet tooth, simply double the amount of white sugar in the dough and then sprinkle sugar on top rather than salt.

Warm the 200 ml of water up to 45°C and then pour the yeast in. Stir until it's dissolved and let it sit for 10 minutes.

In a large mixing bowl, combine the flour, 80 g of sugar and 1 tsp of salt. Once it's thoroughly mixed, make a little well in the centre and pour in the oil and the yeast. Again, mix thoroughly and it should form a dough. If you notice it's getting a bit dry, add a tiny bit more water.

Knead the dough for around 8 minutes when it should be smooth. Get another large bowl and lightly oil its surface. Put the dough in and roll it around to cover it in oil. Cover the bowl and leave it for an hour in a warm place – it should double in size.

Preheat the oven to 220°C and dissolve the baking soda in the hot water. Take the dough out and split it into 8 equal parts. On a floured surface, roll and twist the dough into a pretzel shape. Have fun with it. Nobody's going to judge you.

When you're satisfied aesthetically, dip the pretzels into the baking soda and water solution and then pop them on to a baking tray. Sprinkle with the remaining salt.

Put them in the oven for around 8 minutes and then take them out to serve.

apple crunch

I can't claim this to be a recipe, but my editor agreed that it had to be included to pay a fitting tribute to two of the greatest *Breaking Bad* characters; two men who could hold the attention of the camera for entire scenes without even speaking; two men who I sure as hell wouldn't like to come across on a dark New Mexican night. Or a bright New Mexican afternoon for that matter. These are two scary motherfuckers.

This particular scene typified what was so glorious about Marco and Leonel Salamanca – perfect silence, perfect killers, and they don't look half-bad while they are doing it.

SERVES 1

1 delicious, crunchy red apple
1 policeman, preferably tribal
1 axe
1 homicidal maniac of a brother
1 murdered old woman

Wait for the policeman to arrive on the scene of the previous murder and notice the dead old woman. The chances are he will become agitated. That's fine; stay cool.

Take an apple from the house and appear in the doorway. Wait for him to notice you and stare at him nonchalantly. Note: at this point make sure that your brother is sneaking around the back of the policeman with the axe. If he isn't, this recipe is doomed to fail and the apple will be decidedly less crunchy. More than most recipes, timing is the key to this, and if you get it wrong, then consequences are worse than dry meat, or a cake failing to rise, or even, dare I say it, impure meth.

As your brother approaches, raise the apple to your mouth. When he brings the axe down, take a bite. There should be a very satisfying crunch.

the doghouse

The Doghouse is one of Jesse's favourite diners and it's one of the hotspots for his illicit late-night deals – notably to pick up a gun in the first episode of Season 2. It's also where Walter spends most of the time during *Breaking Bad*... HA! Get it? Because Skyler's always mad at him. With jokes this good I'm surprised I wasn't asked to be a script writer on *Breaking Bad*.

Anyway, The Doghouse is famed, unsurprisingly, for its fantastic hot dogs, which is what keeps bringing Jesse back. That, and the demand for meth. But this recipe focuses more on the hot dogs than the meth.

SERVES 1

1 hot dog
1 hot dog bun
Condiments
Crisps
1 avocado
1 tbsp salsa
1tbsp coriander
1 tsp lemon juice
1 tsp pepper
½ tsp salt
Chili P (optional)

Note: the majority of this method is to do with making guacamole. It's very simple, but do you know what's even simpler? Going to a supermarket and buying some guacamole. But don't worry, I know how much 'foodies' like making life hard for themselves, so here's a quick recipe which includes full instructions on guacamole making.

Cut the avocado in half and remove the seed. Scoop out the avocado from its skin and put it in a mixing bowl. Mash the avocado up, but leave a few lumps.

Add the lemon juice, salt, pepper, coriander and Chili P (if required) and stir it all in.

Pour some water in a saucepan and bring it to boil. Pop the hot dog in and turn the heat down to a medium heat so it simmers. Cook for around 5 minutes and then remove from the pan. Put it in the hot dog bun, and add condiments to taste. Hot dog toppings can actually be quite complex and come in all sorts of varieties – unfortunately, The Doghouse caters for those of simple tastes, so you have to make do with a choice of ketchup, mustard, brown sauce, mayonnaise and chili sauce.

Open the packet of crisps and pour them out into a bowl.

Add the salsa to the guacamole and stir in. Serve as a dip on the side.

office churros

Do you ever go to the kitchen at work and reach for the biscuits or the fruit bowl and think 'I wish there was something more interesting to eat'? Well if so, you're in luck, because there is! And not only is it more interesting, it's also incredibly tasty and very good for you (according to no scientists, anywhere). The traditional Spanish snack (or possibly Chinese... the origin is very murky), the churro, is great to eat anywhere at any time of day.

And because I like it so much, I'm even going to give you a recipe for a chocolate dipping sauce to go with it. Although dipping in tea is always an option as well, and a great English tradition that should not be messed with, so feel free to just stick with that.

SERVES 4

1 litre vegetable oil
500 ml water
120 g white sugar
200 g dark chocolate
200 g flour
100 ml double cream
100 ml milk
6 tbsp golden syrup
4 tsp cinnamon
1 tsp vanilla extract
1 tsp salt

Combine the water, 80 g of sugar, the salt, the vanilla extract and 60 ml of vegetable oil in a saucepan and put it over a high heat. Bring it to the boil and then turn the heat off.

Sift the flour into a large mixing bowl and then make a well in the centre of it. Pour the mixture in and stir vigorously until it forms a smooth ball

Put the chocolate, cream, milk and syrup into another saucepan and put it over a medium to high heat to melt everything. As it's melting, stir the mixture and everything should combine to create a smooth chocolate sauce. Turn the heat down very low to keep the sauce warm.

Pour the remains of the oil into a saucepan and heat on a high heat until sizzling hot. If you have a piping bag, now would be a great time to dig it out and use it to feed the dough into the oil. If not, try and mould the dough into thin churro-stick shapes and drop them into the hot oil.

Leave to fry for a few minutes until they are golden brown all over (timings depend on size, so best to just watch for it). Remove the churros with a slotted spoon and leave them to drain on a paper towel.

Combine the remaining sugar with the cinnamon and sprinkle on to the churros quite liberally. Take the chocolate sauce off of the heat and prepare to serve up.

lily of the valley

And after all that bother, it wasn't ricin that poisoned him at all! Just a simple handful of Lily of the Valley berries – fresh, aromatic, tasty, and just the tiniest bit lethal. A simple mistake that anyone could have made who was a little bit hungry out in the garden and thought they would supplement their diet with some sweet, juicy, organic berries. Maybe he had some help picking them out... maybe he didn't. It's not for me to point any fingers. But I will point you in the way of some Lily of the Valley berries – and I'm sure you won't regret them.

SERVES 1

Lily of the Valley berries
1 hospital
Activated charcoal
IV fluids
Breathing support

Note: The eagle-eyed among you will have spotted that the adjacent photograph is not of Lily of the Valley. My gardening is even worse than my cooking and my Lily of the Valley plant died long before it produced fruit.

Grow the Lily of the Valley plant in your garden. Talk to your local garden centre to find out the best way of doing this – I'm a cook, not a horticulturalist. However, it's a pretty easy plant to grow if you live in a reasonable temperate climate, so this shouldn't be a problem for even the least green-fingered among you.

Wait until the plant has grown berries.
Pick the berries.

Eat the berries.
Check yourself into the nearest hospital and wait for diarrhoea, vomiting, headaches, skin rashes, disorientation and possibly death.
Hopefully, the doctors will prescribe the charcoal and get you on the IV before the breathing support becomes too much of an issue. I hear that isn't too comfortable.

'how are you even alive?'

If you're off on a weekend away, whether it be with your mates, or on a cook or with your family, you always want to think ahead and bring a survival food pack with you. And you can't do better than Jesse's 'How Are You Even Alive?' which he showcases in Season 2 Episode 9, much to Walter's disgust but, I like to think, also his secret pleasure. Because ultimately, who could say no to a pack like this?

And sure, Jesse could have brought more water. And yes, he didn't need to throw all the water they had over the malfunctioning motor. But I still maintain that his suggestion of breaking the RV down into parts to build a dune buggy that could dune buggy them right out of the desert was valid and that Walter should have been taken it much more seriously.

SERVES 2

**6 bags Cheetos – you can
never have enough Cheetos
3 bags Funyuns
2 bags Gummy Bears
Assorted other crisps and
sweets as taste dictates
10 gallons water**

Take the bags of sweets and crisps and pack into a large bag or box.

Transport that bag or box with you, along with the 10 gallons of water, to whatever your destination is.

Chow down as and when you are hungry.

Note: don't worry about nutrition. When cooking and/or taking meth, if *Breaking Bad* is anything to go by, your diet is most likely the least of your problems.

jesse pinkman

Jesse... oh, Jesse. Jesse Pinkman has to be one of the most popular characters who has ever appeared on TV. And probably the only character whose fans beg him to call them a bitch.

He first appears as a dysfunctional minor-league meth cook obsessed with Chili P who escapes from the DEA by jumping out of a window – from the bosom of an attractive young girl and right into Walter White's clutches. Thus began a partnership (and surrogate father-son relationship) that lasted, through many, many trials and tribulations, the entire length of the series.

As the series goes on, we see Jesse mature into one of the greatest cooks in the country and, not only that, a cook with a conscience. His constant battle between wanting to do the right thing and having to 'make the right move' wears Jesse down emotionally and causes him to have a number of breakdowns which, ultimately, just make us love him even more.

NICKNAME: Cap'n Cook; Jesse Jackson
OCCUPATION: Crystal meth cook; The Guy
FAVOURITE FOOD: Funyuns. Or anything with Chili P in.
BEST QUOTES:
Jesse to Walt: 'Look, we got, we got an entire lab right here. Alright? How about you pick some of these chemicals and mix up some rocket fuel? That way you could just send up a signal flare. Or you make some kind of robot to get us help, or a homing device, or build a new battery, or... Wait. No. What if we just take some stuff off of the RV and build it into something completely different? You know, like a... Like a dune buggy. That way, we can just dune buggy or...'
Jesse in therapy: 'The thing is, if you just do stuff, and nothing happens, what's it all mean? What's the point?'
Jesse to Walt: 'I got two dudes that turned into raspberry slushie then flushed down my toilet. I can't even take a proper dump in there. I mean, the whole damn house has got to be haunted by now.'
Jesse to Walt: 'You don't need a criminal lawyer. You need a criminal lawyer.'
Jesse to Hank and Steve Gomez: 'Look... look, you two guys are just... guys, okay? Mr White... he's the devil. You know, he is... he is smarter than you, he is luckier than you. Whatever... whatever you think is supposed to happen... I'm telling you, the exact reverse opposite of that is gonna happen, okay?'
Jesse in the scrapyard: 'Yeah, bitch! Magnets!'
Jesse to Walt: 'So you do have a plan! Yeah Mr White! Yeah science!'

chicken nugget dippers

Madrigal Electromotive GmbH has its figurative fingers in a hell of a lot of figurative pies. It deals in heavy machinery, chemical supplies, methamphetamines, construction, shipping… you name it, it does it. But surely nothing can be more lucrative than the Chicken Nugget Dipper trade that it is involved in. Madrigal employs whole teams of top-class scientists in its labs to develop not just the nuggets themselves, but also the dips that go with them. They do everything from improving the traditional ketchup to a new take on barbecue mesquite… to Franch, a half-Ranch, half-French dressing composite (nobody ever said the Germans were very creative). Admittedly, I can't see Walter White working his magic down the lab for them, but I suppose he has better things to do.

Breaking Bad allows us the briefest look at the inner workings of Madrigal before the suicide of one of the briefest cameos of a crime kingpin any show has had.

SERVES 4

900 g chicken
200 g breadcrumbs
125 ml milk
1 egg
1 tsp thyme
Chili P
Wide array of condiments
Fly (optional)

Preheat the oven to 200ºC. Dice the chicken into small 3 cm pieces.

Add the milk to the egg in a large bowl and beat it vigorously. Add the diced chicken to soak for a few minutes. While it's soaking, mix the breadcrumbs with the thyme and Chili P and put the mixture on a baking tray. Remove the chicken from the milky mixture and add the soaked chicken to the breadcrumb mixture. Roll it around until it's thoroughly covered.

Pop the chicken in the oven and let it bake for around 15 minutes.

Serve up with the array of condiments to choose from. The more exotic, the better.

'everyone dies in this movie, don't they?' popcorn

As much as they would both like to, Walt and Walt Jr don't spend all that much quality father and son time together as the series goes on. Whose door the blame for that lies at is none of my business but, like any teenager, Walt Jr probably wants to spend less time with his parents. Oh... and I guess Walt being the greatest meth druglord in the United States of America does cause a few rifts in his relationships with his immediate family.

Fortunately, they do find an opportunity to bond over one of the all-time great movies: *Scarface*. It's perhaps not *Breaking Bad*'s most subtle of allusions and the comparisons between Walt and Tony Montana are fairly obvious to even the most casual observer. So when Walt says 'everyone dies in this movie, don't they?' you do have to wonder just how well things are going to turn out for him... At least he has some popcorn to cheer himself up.

SERVES 2

100 g popcorn kernels
60 ml vegetable oil
50 g butter
Salt

Pour the oil into a deep saucepan and start to heat it on a medium heat. Add 5 kernels to the oil and cover the pan. When you hear them pop, the oil is hot enough to cook.

Add the rest of the kernels and cover the pan again. Remove the pan straight away from the heat and leave for 30 seconds. Return the pan to the heat and the kernels should start popping away.

Wait until the majority of the kernels have popped and then remove the popcorn from the oil with a slotted spoon. Pour the oil away and return the popcorn to the hot, now empty, pan. Immediately slather the butter over the top of the popcorn while it is still hot and leave it to melt. Sprinkle as much salt on as you would like and serve up.

'did i lose a bet?' nachos

If you're feeling like your life is spiralling out of control then the best place to go is a dive bar. Everybody knows that. And what do dive bars do well? Nachos.

So when Hank takes Gomie out for a drink and a quick punch-up in Season 3, he thinks he's doing him a favour when he orders him some nachos to nibble on. Unfortunately, just because something is the best meal in the house, doesn't mean it's going to be a good meal... that depends on the house. And this is a bad house. In fact, it's so bad that Gomie reckons he must have lost a bet to be forced to eat them, but fortunately a fight breaks out before he has to eat too many. Hopefully this recipe will make something marginally nicer:

SERVES 2

120 g tortilla chips
200 g beef mince
150 g salsa
100 g kidney beans
100 g cheese
30 ml water
2 tbsp sour cream
2 tbsp guacamole
1 large onion
1 tbsp tomato purée
½ tbsp olive oil
Chili P

Preheat oven to 200°C. Chop the onion up and grate the cheese. Heat olive oil on medium heat in a frying pan. When hot, cook the onion for 2 minutes and then add the mince. Cook until browned, which should be around 5 minutes.

Add the Chili P, kidney beans, tomato purée and water and cook for another 5 minutes, stirring throughout.

Put the tortilla chips on a baking tray in an artistically pleasing manner. Dump the mince on after the 5 minutes is up. Then, sprinkle it all with cheese – I don't think it's possible to use too much cheese in this recipe and, in fact, it's essential to make sure that the nachos are almost completely covered with the cheese because otherwise they get badly burned in the oven.

Pop it in the oven and take out after 8 minutes. Put the salsa, sour cream and guacamole on top (try not to mix them together at this stage for aesthetic reasons – the different colours are nice, as is convincingly shown by the black-and-white photo opposite) and then serve it up.

fring's business snack pack

Gustavo Fring probably isn't the traditional drug lord; he drives a ten-year-old Volvo. If I was in charge of a 'company' worth almost a billion dollars I might treat myself to something a bit less... looking like it was about to break down.

He's not exactly lavish with his hospitality either. On a number of occasions he hosts 'business meetings' in his HQ – a shoddy, temporary building – but he does at least always make sure there's food available. Even if nobody ever eats any. This could be because it's relatively tricky to feel too comfortable under Gus's intense glare, and I don't think hunger pangs would be the first thing on anyone's mind. But it could also be because, for the owner of a successful chain of delicious fast-food establishments, the culinary treats on offer are so healthy and boring. I don't know anyone who would eat this sort of stuff out of choice.

But if vegetables are your thing, follow this easy recipe for Fring's Business Snack Pack.

SERVES 6

3 carrots
5 celery sticks
½ head of broccoli
200 g cherry tomatoes
1 cucumber
200 g sour cream
250 g mayonnaise
1 tsp dill
1 tsp tarragon
1 tsp parsley
1 tsp chives

In a mixing bowl, combine the sour cream, mayonnaise, dill, tarragon, parsley, chives and stir thoroughly. Add salt, pepper and Chili P to taste. This is your dip.

Chop the carrots, celery sticks, cucumber and broccoli into bite size pieces. The cherry tomatoes are already in bite-size pieces.

Serve up in a Snack Pack platter with the dip in the middle. Make sure you clingfilm it so that the vegetables are still fresh when everyone you offer them to turns them down.

Best served with: tea and coffee, slightly bizarrely, but that's what Fring serves, and he's the boss. If you have the guts, add ricin to the coffee to taste.

desserts

Although *Breaking Bad* has a preference for the spicy, the sweet gets a look-in on occasion as well. Which is excellent, because there's only so much Chili P one person can eat, although Jesse might not believe me. And very few dessert recipes call for Chili P, no matter what Jesse tries to tell you.

'Sometimes forbidden fruit tastes the sweetest' –
HANK SCHRADER

(your legs are like) jelly

Hospital food doesn't have the greatest reputation as food goes, but it's very difficult to mess up jelly – or jello as our American counterparts would have us believe it's called. Hank, however, passes up the little treat with disdain, and one can only imagine it's because the wobbly mess on his plate reminds him of the wobbly mess his legs have become.

Whatever his reason for not eating, it looked delicious to me, and here's a great way to make fresh jelly with real strawberries. And I'm even throwing in the option of adding a dash (or more) of vodka for you hedonists out there.

SERVES 6

220 g caster sugar
700 ml water
500 g strawberries
10 g powdered gelatine
A tipple of vodka (optional)

Pour the sugar and 650 ml of water into a saucepan and bring it to boil on a high heat. Turn the heat down and leave to simmer for around 5 minutes.

Wash and de-stalk the strawberries. Put them in a blender and blend into a fine pulp. Pour the pulp into a large bowl and then pour the syrupy mixture over it. Add the vodka at this point – nobody will judge you for how much you put in. And if they do, they are probably not worth being friends with, so it doesn't matter.

Leave to rest for around 30 minutes and then pass the mixture through a sieve to remove any seeds. Unless you like a seedy jelly.

Add the gelatine to the remaining water and leave it for 5 minutes. Then, take around 200 ml of the syrup mixture and pour into a saucepan, along with the gelatine mixture. Heat on a low to medium heat and stir until the gelatine has dissolved. Pour back into the syrup mixture and stir to mix it in.

If you have a jelly mould, pour in the mixture and put the mould in the fridge to set. If you don't, just put the bowl in the fridge to set. This should take around 4 hours, so I hope you've read to the end of this recipe before you started, otherwise it won't be ready in time for dessert.

the waffle house

After being held in a police cell for hours the chances are that you will be feeling tired, a bit cranky, possibly with low blood-sugar levels, a rumbling stomach and maybe even a craving for a hit of something a bit stronger. And, to be honest, even if I haven't been held in a police cell I often struggle with these issues – which is why one of the greatest places on earth is The Waffle House. They serve waffles there.

So it is unsurprising that Jesse takes Wendy there to thank her for providing him with an alibi while he was up to some slightly nefarious activities.

SERVES 2

80 g flour
80 g butter
120 ml milk
1 egg
1 tsp baking powder
½ tsp icing sugar
½ tsp vanilla extract
A pinch of salt
Maple syrup

Sift the flour into a mixing bowl with the baking powder, sugar and salt. On a low heat, melt the butter in a frying pan and add the vanilla, the milk and the egg yolk (separate from the white) to the mixing bowl. Give it a good stir until it is a smooth batter.

Beat the egg white and then fold it into the batter.

Turn on your waffle iron – you really need one to make waffles I'm afraid. If you don't have one, they are awesome. Go out and buy one, you won't regret it – and wait until it's hot.

Pour the batter in and close the waffle iron. Cook until a delicious golden brown – it should only be a minute or so.

Repeat until all the batter is gone.

Lavishly slather maple syrup all over the waffles. I like to do it until the waffle is more of a transport mechanism to get the maple syrup to my mouth, rather than a meal in itself. But each to their own.

peekabun

Jesse's going to be a great dad one day – that's obvious. He's loving and caring and under his watchful eye Brock only nearly died once, so he knows what he's doing. Admittedly he can get a bit unstable and depressed at times... but who among us can say they haven't gone a bit off the rails every so often and thrown week-long parties for meth-heads they've never met before, eh?

When Jesse comes across a malnourished little kid with an unhealthy fixation over TV shopping channels he feels sorry for him – even though he's ginger – and they play an extended game of peekaboo. He even pops out to get him something to eat and grabs him an iced bun to gobble down. Who needs vegetables, am I right? Definitely not a kid on the verge of developing rickets.

SERVES 2

250 g white flour
40 g caster sugar
25 g butter
1 egg
7 g dried yeast
1 tsp salt
100 ml milk
100 g icing sugar
2–3 tsp water
1 tsp lemon juice

Preheat the oven to 220ºC.

Sift the flour and salt into a large mixing bowl and then add the butter, sugar and dried yeast. Mix it together and make a well in the centre. In a separate bowl, beat the egg, add the milk and then pour into the well in the dry mixture.

Mix it all together with your hands and get kneading. Once it becomes dough-like, put it on to a floured surface and carry on kneading for around 10 minutes until the dough is light and fluffy. This is very important unless you like iced ciabatta buns. If you notice it's getting a bit dry you can add a touch more milk.

Put the dough back in the bowl, cover it and leave it for an hour or so, until it rises to double the size.

Return to the dough and divide it into 6 equal pieces. On the floured surface, knead the individual pieces into long bun shapes. Place the buns on a baking tray and then cover again and leave for a further 30 minutes to rise. Leave enough space in between them that they can double in size; overcrowding can be an issue.

Put them in the oven and bake them for 10 minutes. They'll rise even further at this point, but now it's OK if they're bumping against each other.

While they are baking, make the icing. Feel free to make more than the recipe calls for and eat straight from the bowl.

Not nutritious, but delicious.

Sift the icing sugar into a bowl and add the lemon juice with 2–3tsp of water, depending on how thick you like your icing. Mix together until you have a thick paste.

Wait for the buns to cool slightly and then spoon the icing on top.

fro yo, bitch!

Although fro yo (frozen yoghurt) hasn't really made the leap across the Pond as yet, in America it's an incredibly popular dessert. Why, I don't know... it will always be the poor man's ice cream in my eyes. But Fro Yo, Bitch! is a great way to cool you down and calm your nerves on a warm New Mexican afternoon, especially if you've just been involved in (read: intentionally caused) a serious car crash. No Walt, he definitely didn't come out of nowhere.

Obviously, the beauty of Fro Yo, Bitch! is that it can come in pretty much any different flavour. If you're English, that means vanilla, strawberry and chocolate – just like ice cream, we don't experiment. If it's not part of the traditional Neapolitan ice cream, it's not worth having. But if you're American then there are literally hundreds, if not thousands, of flavour combinations. I'm a vanilla man, though, so that's what we're having.

SERVES 4

750 g Greek yoghurt
200 ml skimmed milk
180 g white sugar
1 tsp vanilla extract

Mix the yoghurt, milk, sugar and vanilla extract together in a large mixing bowl. If you have an ice cream maker (why would you?) then simply refrigerate for 45 minutes and then use the ice cream maker to whip up the frozen yoghurt as per usual.

If you are a normal person who buys their ice cream at the store, put the mixture into a bowl or dish, cover it with foil and pop it into the freezer. Freeze for around 2 hours and then take it out and give it a vigorous beating until it's soft again.

Repeat this process 1 or 2 more times depending on how fluffy you want the Fro Yo, Bitch! to be.

Note: this really just tastes like cold yoghurt with a bit of vanilla, but have no fear because other flavours are bloody easy. For chocolate, for example, all you need is to replace the vanilla with 3 tbsp of cocoa powder. And for those even more adventurous than that, the sky is your limit. Second note: I still don't get why people prefer this to ice cream.

blue crystal

Disastrously, after a lengthy legal battle, it was ruled that this book could not contain a recipe for cooking up a batch of crystal meth, even though *Breaking Bad* has conclusively proven that nothing that terrible can come of it. I tried in vain to argue that the events of *Breaking Bad* showed that the process and consequences of a good cook were exciting and character-forming but, alas, the courts disagreed.

So I am publishing instead the very next best thing – a simple recipe for Blue Crystal rock candy which will BLOW YOUR MIND! This stuff is pure, man, and it kicks like a mule.

SERVES 8

180 ml water
600 g sugar
320 g golden syrup
2 tsp vanilla extract (or any other flavour you choose)
Blue food colouring
Chili P (optional – damages the purity)
1 sugar thermometer (essential to obtain high purity. This is a science)

Prepare a baking tray by covering it in a non-stick baking sheet.

Mix the water, sugar and syrup together in a saucepan and put it over a medium to high heat. While it is heating add the vanilla extract, blue colouring and Chili P (optional) and stir in until a splendid blue colour is achieved.

Bring it to the boil and stop stirring. Add the candy thermometer and watch carefully until the temperature reaches 150°C. This temperature might be labelled 'hard crack' which is exactly what we are hoping to achieve. If your crystal doesn't reach this temperature then it will not solidify properly – and the entire batch while be ruined!

Take the mixture off the heat and let it cool. It should be bubbling. When the bubbles stop breaking the surface of the liquid, pour immediately on to the baking tray and allow it to cool.

Use a small hammer to break the crystal into shards and check for purity.

It's not quite as good as the real thing, but at least this batch can be enjoyed by the whole family.

lydia rodarte-quayle

Ms Rodarte-Quayle is a highly successful executive at Madrigal Electromotive GmbH and, from her position of power as the Head of Logistics there, is able to maintain control over a large network of criminal activity. Nervous and with a phobia of blood and violence, the single mother isn't the most obvious of criminal kingpins. But, as Mike knew all along, looks can be deceiving, and Lydia should be underestimated at your peril.

When Lydia first appears on the scene, it is easy to pity her as someone who is maybe just in over her head. Her penchant for killing a dozen people at a time if they are a threat to either her safety or her profit margins swiftly does away with that impression, though. Although generally quite cold and calculating, Lydia was one half of one of the potentially more bizarre relationships that was just beginning to bear romantic fruit when *Breaking Bad* reached its incredible conclusion. The will-they won't-they between Todd and Lydia was shaping up to be very interesting... I suppose now we will never know what might have been.

NICKNAME: Nobody would ever give Lydia a nickname
OCCUPATION: Executive at Madrigal Electromotive GmbH (Head of Logisitics)
FAVOURITE FOOD: Stevia sweetener
BEST QUOTES:
Lydia to Walt: 'Is it done? Is he gone?'
Lydia on meeting Jesse: 'Sorry, but I'm not gonna apologize for being careful – with all that's been happening, for all I knew you were one of those undercover people they send into high schools, so, yeah, I'll take paranoid any day over getting gang-raped by prison guards.'

the classic

On hearing the news that a loved one is in remission, what better way to celebrate than with a classic American dessert of apple pie and ice cream? Of course, almost everyone around the table actually wishes Walt was dead – they just don't know it yet. But The Classic is so good that we can just glaze over that little issue and enjoy the good hearty All-American dessert they are eating.

And yes, I am going to provide a recipe for vanilla ice cream but you should really just go to the store. You can get a litre of vanilla soft-scoop for a couple of quid, and it's delicious. There's really no need to go to the trouble of making your own when it's more expensive and probably, let's face it, going to turn out worse. And while you're at the store, you might as well pick up an apple pie.

If you do insist on making it, here's what you need.

SERVES 6

Pie crust: 225 g butter
50 g caster sugar
2 eggs
350 g flour
Pie filling: 1 kg baking apples
120 g sugar (can be white or brown sugar, or even a mix of the two)
2 tbsp butter
1 tbsp corn flour
1 tbsp lemon juice

If you have an ice cream maker then the ice cream is relatively easy (see Fro Yo, Bitch! for comments on ice cream makers). Just mix the ingredients together – only use the egg yolks though, not the whites. And obviously don't just chuck the vanilla pod in. Remove the seeds and use just them – and pour the mixture into the ice cream maker. If you don't, then things are slightly trickier.

Milk doesn't do well in ice cream unless it's well churned, so replace the milk with cream. Pour the litre of cream into a saucepan and add the vanilla (seeds or extract). Heat over a high heat until boiling.

Turn the heat down very low and add the sugar and salt, stirring until they're dissolved. Crack the eggs into a bowl but remove the egg whites. Whisk the yolks and then add to the cream mixture. Give it another little whisk until it's well and truly mixed.

Pour the mixture into a container that can go in the freezer and pop it in. It should

1 tsp cinnamon
¼ tsp nutmeg
pinch salt
Ice cream: 500 ml cream
500 ml full fat milk (or more
cream. See method for
details)
3 vanilla pods (alternatively
6 tsp vanilla extract)
160 g caster sugar
3 eggs
pinch salt

be set and be ready to go in around 3 hours.

Warning: this is intensely creamy ice cream. It's more like cream of ice cream. It is still, however, delicious.

The pie: If they aren't already, peel, core and slice the baking apples into small slices, about 1 cm thick. In a large mixing bowl, mix the apple slices, sugar, salt, corn flour, cinnamon and nutmeg. Leave it for 1 hour.

To make the pie crust, beat the butter and sugar in a large mixing bowl. When it's well mixed, crack one egg in, along with the yolk of the other (keep the white separate for later). Briefly beat again before slowly mixing in the flour. Work it with your hands until it's become dough and then roll it into a ball. Pop it into the fridge for around 30 minutes.

Pre-heat the oven to 190ºC. When the apples are ready, pour from the bowl into a colander and catch the liquid in a saucepan. There should be about 100 ml there. Heat over a medium heat until just under half has boiled off so that there's

60 ml or so left. Pour the syrup back over the apples.

Take out the pastry. Cut ⅓ off and set aside, then line your pie tin with the rest of it. Hang the crust slightly over the edge. Roll the remaining pastry out to make a circle with a diameter 6 cm greater than the pie tin.

Move the apple mixture into the pie and sprinkle the lemon juice over the top. Also, dot the butter around on top of the mixture so that it melts evenly when cooked.

Put the lid over the top of the mixture and crimp the edges down to seal the pie goodness inside. Trim the edges so it is even and then make a few slashes in the top so that the steam can escape while baking.

Brush the egg white over the pie and sprinkle some sugar over the top of the crust to give it some extra sweet crunchiness.

Bake it for 40 minutes and serve up with your delicious home-made (if you're foolhardy enough to have made it) vanilla ice cream.

congratulations, you've killed someone! have a cake

There's quite a good chance that most of you reading this won't have ever shot anyone. Or, if you have, then you probably won't have shot them to death. But for those of you who have, you'll know that you haven't been to a party until you've been to one celebrating a successful shootout.

When Hank came back to the police station after his shootout at the beginning of Season 2 he probably wasn't expecting anything too special. Little did he know that, as soon as word came in on the radio that he'd taken his target down, the office began planning for his return.

One integral part of this merriment is, of course, the cake – and this particular one didn't disappoint. As you should know from reading modern etiquette books, the correct cake to make in this circumstance is chocolate – with a portrait of the shooter, in this case Hank, holding a smoking gun made out of the icing. This cake, though artistically suspect, met all expectations.

SERVES 6

200 g flour
200 g caster sugar
150 g butter
100 ml milk
80 g cocoa powder
3 eggs
2 tsp vanilla extract

Preheat the oven to 180°C. Add the flour, sugar, baking powder and bicarbonate of soda together in a large mixing bowl and stir vigorously to combine. Add the butter and beat vigorously until well combined.

In a separate bowl, mix the milk, cocoa powder, eggs and vanilla extract together and whisk thoroughly.

Pour the liquid mixture into the dry ingredients and beat it thoroughly.

Grease the two cake tins with butter and pour the mixture equally into the two of them. Pop them into the oven and leave for 30 minutes or so.

In a large mixing bowl, combine the butter and the icing sugar with an electric whisk on low speed. If you don't have an electric whisk, then you'd better have a

1 tsp baking powder
1 tsp bicarbonate soda
Icing: 500 g icing sugar
160 g butter
25 ml full fat milk
2 tsp vanilla extract
Note: you need 2 cake tins
with a 20 cm diameter and
removable bases for this
recipe. And an electric whisk
comes in handy too.

strong wrist.

Slowly add the milk and vanilla extract and whisk as you go. The speed should now be on high in order to make the icing light and fluffy. If you are manually whisking... good luck. The longer you whisk, the lighter and fluffier the icing will be, so stop when you are happy.

When the cakes are done, remove from the oven and leave to cool for about 5 minutes. Spread the icing over one cake and then stack the other on top and spread more icing all over them.

To decorate: decorating a cake can be very rewarding if you put the time in to do it, and to complete this recipe you really do need to get the artistic juices flowing. However, there are just so many different ways about it that I've decided to introduce an 'interactive' element to this cookbook:
1) Turn on your computer
2) Open your preferred web browser
3) Go to www.google.co.uk (or similar)
4) Type in 'icing cake decoration help' (or similar)

5) Learn how to decorate a cake
In no way am I being lazy about this – it's important you understand that – I'm simply giving you the opportunity to develop and expand a new skill set.

Note: if a cake makes a good party, then presents make a great one. But what do you get for someone like Hank who has just come out on top in a shooting competition? Don't worry, *Breaking Bad* has all the answers for you.

What better way to celebrate a spot of killing than grabbing a trophy from the body... just a little something to remember them by. So pop down to the mortuary and see what's on offer – ideally something distinctive like a glass eye, a silver set of gnashers or a fake leg. But if nothing obvious presents itself, or the mortician is being awkward about things, then another great opportunity is at the funeral, when stealing what you can from the coffin is a must. This gift is perfect and definitely not insensitive, morbid and downright disgusting.

steven gomez

Gomez was given the tricky task of having to be Hank's partner in the DEA. While Hank's a good cop, he can be a little bit excitable and obsessive, and Gomez has to deal with that and keep it in check. Later, when ASAC Schrader is in charge at the DEA, Gomez is not only the one who looks after him and stops him from making too many mistakes because of his obsession with Heisenberg, but he's also the friend he turns to when the going gets rough.

Unlucky, Gomez.

And even more unlucky for Gomie is the fact that, because he is obviously of Mexican heritage, Hank throws a decent amount of banter towards him throughout the seasons which is borderline racist. Fortunately, Gomie can give as good as he gets, and he has the added advantage of being able to insult Hank in a language he won't even understand.

NICKNAME: Gomie
OCCUPATION: Agent at the DEA
FAVOURITE FOOD: Los Hermanos Pollos – especially when free
BEST QUOTES:
Gomie to Hank: 'Tuco wasn't my homie any more than Charlie Manson was yours.'
Hank: 'Alright, some of you already know my brother-in-law. He's a good man. The doctors are saying this operation has a real chance of helping him... Biggest donation gets a six-pack of my very own Schraderbräu. Home brewed to silky perfection.'
Gomie: 'Smallest donation gets two six-packs.'
Gomie to Hank: 'If your guy had his meeting at KFC, you wouldn't immediately assume that he's sitting down with Colonel Sanders.'

Note: This list is by no means exhaustive. There are plenty of other occasions on *Breaking Bad* when alcoholic drinks are consumed, and plenty more when they should have been, but weren't. This is just a guide and you may instead want to go through my checklist to see if drinking an alcoholic drink is appropriate:

Are you awake?

If the answer is yes, then treat yourself.

'Free food always tastes good. Free drinks... even better' –
HANK SCHRADER

drinks

While a fair amount of drinking goes on in *Breaking Bad* there isn't, with a couple of notable exceptions, all that much that would require a recipe. Therefore, to call this a recipe list would be misleading; this is more of a guide to when and in what mood it is appropriate to drink which drink.

Moreover, although plenty of non-alcoholic drinks are consumed over the course of the show, they just don't count in my eyes. Therefore, this list will be exclusively alcoholic. So, for any under-18s who may be reading this, take careful note so that, when you go out under-age drinking, you make sure that you are doing it right.

the winst

'To clean cars and clean money' was the toast that Walter White and Skyler clinked to when celebrating buying their dirty new car wash. Having tricked the unfortunate Bogdan into selling up, the Whites were now the proud new owners of the A1 Car Wash (which gave rise to possibly the worst marketing slogan ever: 'Have an A1 day'. What does that even mean? I expected better from those two) and Skyler had graduated to cooking her own books, rather than Ted Beneke's.

To celebrate in style, Walter turned to a great Englishman for help, Winston Churchill, and bought his favourite champagne, the Pol Roger, at a snip for only $320. Well, that's a snip for someone earning several million a year but, as Skyler points out, not so affordable for an unemployed teacher who has just shelled out his entire life-savings on a car wash. Fortunately, they decided it was best to 'destroy the evidence', so that fine champagne certainly didn't go to waste.

SERVES 2

Moods:
Celebration. Profligacy.

Any champagne will do (Cava, anyone?), but the more expensive the better. You're celebrating, after all.

Always open with a satisfying pop and try to subtly aim the cork towards the other person without making it obvious that's what you are doing. If you hit them, pour yourself a little extra.

Absolutely no shaking of the bottle to be allowed before opening. Any foamy champagne that sprays from the bottle upon opening is less champagne in your belly.

Best served chilled in champagne flutes. Pour a little in first and let the bubbles die down before topping up the rest of the glass.

'chasing monsters'

In Season 5 Episode 8, shortly before a little revelation, Hank invites Walter to have a drink with him, even though he knows Walt's driving, and the last time I checked the police were meant to be pretty hot on that not happening. But that's a measure of just how depressed Hank is feeling – there's just been a series of unfortunate accidents for him in a handful of prisons and times are hard for Hank just at the moment.

Luckily, there's no better way to cheer yourself up than some heavy afternoon drinking – that's been scientifically proven to be a fact – so Hank pours himself and Walt a couple of Bourbon whiskeys. While they are drinking Hank does a serious bit of self-reflection, which doesn't come naturally to him so you know it must be important. Apparently, when Hank was a kid he had a job marking up trees that were due to be cut down and, though you might think it was quite nice wandering around in the woods all day for a living, it actually wasn't. Still, 'tagging trees is a lot better than chasing monsters.'

It's a bit harsh calling Walt a monster right to his face like that, but I think even he would say Hank's got a valid point.

SERVES 2

Moods:
Nostalgia. Despair. Over-whelming sense of self-doubt and loathing.

Bourbon whiskey is best served at room temperature in glass tumblers.

It can be either on the rocks, meaning with ice (Walt), or straight, if you're feeling either very macho or very depressed. I would hazard a guess that, with Hank, it is the latter at that particular point in time.

hank's remission margaritas

Walter's in remission and everyone's happy. Except maybe Walter, who seems more angry than anything – there's just no pleasing some people. But Hank knows how to please the people, and there's no better way to do that than a round of Hank's famed Remission Margaritas. When he cracks these out at the start of the party, everyone's happy, laughing and life is good. This is the good side of tequila.

Later, Hank, Walt and Walt Jr are sitting around enjoying a quiet drink by themselves around the pool. Things get a bit out of hand: Walt Jr has a couple more shots of straight tequila than he should, Walt makes a tit out of himself and semi-ruins the party, and then Walt Jr is a little sick in the pool and completely ruins it. This is the bad side of tequila.

SERVES 4

Moods:
Happiness. Party-time

You need 160 ml of tequila, 100 ml of lime juice, 80 ml of Cointreau, a couple of limes, a few ice cubes and some salt.

Cut the limes into slices and then pour the tequila, lime juice and Cointreau into a cocktail shaker with the ice cubes and shake hard. After 20 seconds or so, pour the mixture through a strainer into the glasses. Add some ice cubes, rub the salt along the rim of the glass and stick a lime slice on the rim.

Stay away from straight tequila.

hank schrader

ASAC Schrader is a real man's man – he fights crime, brews beer, hosts barbecues... collects minerals... and he does it all with a smile on his face and a ribald joke on his lips. Although he's often dealing with very serious issues like drugs, illness, death or paralysis, Hank, with his boisterous personality, refuses to let the world see that it bothers him.

However, behind closed doors ASAC Schrader can be a different person entirely. He tries to mask his own weaknesses, especially when he begins to suffer from panic attacks, and, much like Walt, he refuses to accept help from anybody. It is only when he reaches the lowest of the low that he finally lets Marie in to help him emotionally – and they become quite the formidable team.

Although he can sometimes be curt and even rude to those he loves the most (mainly Marie), there's no doubting that Hank cares deeply for his family and would do anything, well almost anything, to look after them. Ultimately, though, Hank is an ASAC first and foremost, and his career and reputation means everything to him.

NICKNAME: ASAC Schrader
OCCUPATION: ASAC of the DEA office in Albuquerque
FAVOURITE FOOD: The White Cookout
BEST QUOTES:
Hank to Jack: 'My name is ASAC Schrader, and you can go fuck yourself.'
Jesse: 'So what're you saying? Like, I shot someone with, like, a gun?'
Hank: 'You? No. Only shooting that you do is into a Kleenex.'
Hank to Heisenberg: 'It was you. All along, it was you! You son of a bitch. You drove into traffic to keep me from that laundry. That call I got telling me Marie was in the hospital... that wasn't Pinkman. You had my cell number. You killed ten witnesses to save your sorry ass. You bombed a nursing home. Heisenberg. Heisenberg! You lying, two-face sack of shit.'
Hank to Marie: 'What I did to Pinkman... that's not who I'm supposed to be. All this, everything that's happened, I swear to God, Marie, I think the universe is trying to tell me something and I'm finally ready to listen. I'm just not the man I thought I was. I think I'm done as a cop.'

salud

Remember that time I warned you to stay away from straight tequila? Well this is why: Zafiro Anejo. For tequila lovers this is perfection, a well-aged tequila from the blue agave plant and even the bottle is a work of art. When you take a sip of it, it's like you're sipping the heart and soul of Mexico itself.

Unfortunately for the cartel, alcohol can be dangerous, and especially so when it's served up by Gustavo Fring. After all the times Gus was meant to be poisoned by Jesse, with one word, 'Salud', he does Jesse's job for him. Whatever else you can say about him, you can't deny that Gus isn't good at taking revenge, especially when served cold.

SERVES: A cartel-full

Moods:
Business. Homicide.

This shouldn't be sipped but taken as a shot all at once, and only after the customary 'Salud'.

Always wait for someone else to drink first, so you can be sure it isn't poisoned. Also, double-check that they haven't taken an antidote at any point prior to the drinking.

If you are poisoning the tequila, ensure that you use a colourless and tasteless poison, because if this is the last thing that someone is going to drink then you don't want to ruin it for them.

schraderbräu

For generations (at least one, anyway), the Schraders have been brewing their own beer, Schraderbräu, to provide the fine citizens of New Mexico with the ultimate experience in beer drinking. Not only does Hank have an excellent home-brewing kit in his garage, he also has a couple of taps with a bottling system – and a snazzy logo which encapsulates everything we love about the man, the legend, ASAC Hank Schrader.

Who could have foreseen that in a show about cooking crystal meth, the true genius would be the brother-in-law brewing beer in his own house? And yet Schraderbräu is perennially popular and in high demand, possibly because it is brewed to silky perfection. If Prohibition was still in force in the USA then *Breaking Bad* would have been a very different show, and Hank would have been a lot richer.

It's impossible to recreate the glories of Schraderbräu exactly unfortunately, particularly because, as Hank himself points out, 'Brewing is an art form, Marie. The Christmas batch of '06? Come on...' However, it's more than possible to try brewing your own beer for yourself. And what's the worst that can happen – no matter how bad you are at it, you are still going to end up with drinkable alcohol.

SERVES: The masses

Moods:
All occasions

There are a number of kits sold online that could get you started on your first foray into the brewing world, but if you want to go it alone this is the bare minimum of what you will need:
a large pot (to hold the beer – size is dependent on ambition); an airtight fermenting bucket; an airlock and stopper (to attach to the bucket above); tubing and clamps (to bottle the beer with); a bottle filler; bottles; bottle caps; a bottle capper; a cool logo design and printer (to print off aforementioned cool logo design).

Once you have the equipment, you need the ingredients. Again, it's easiest to look online and search for yourself, because

every beer uses different ratios, but effectively you will need malt, hops, yeast and sugar, plus anything that you want to flavour it. An easy ale might consist of: 2.5 kg unhopped malt extract; 70 g hops; 1 pack of liquid yeast; 150 g sugar.

Typically you would brew the beer by boiling the malt and the hops in water for around 1 hour, and you would put in other flavours at this stage.

Allow the mixture to cool to room temperature when you should add more water to it until it fills your fermenter and, once the mixture reaches room temperature again, you can add the yeast.

The beer should then ferment for around 2 weeks in the airtight fermenter. The beer should then be siphoned through tubing to another container where corn flour is added, and then siphoned into bottles, which are capped.

The beer is then left to age for around 6 weeks (or more!) and over this time it will also become carbonated.

Slap the logos on to the bottle and, when you think the beer is aged enough, refrigerate.

Open and enjoy with friends as an ice-cold refreshment.

This takes a while, months in fact, and while I am normally against spending ages doing something when you could just buy it at the store, I am all for home-brewing. Just look how happy Hank is when he's spending time with his beloved Schraderbräu.

Note: while ageing, the yeast is still fermenting in the bottle and, as a consequence of its anaerobic respiration, it is producing a fair amount of carbon dioxide. This gives the beer its bubbles, which is obviously a good thing.

However, if you are of a nervous disposition and think it possible that someone might be willing to break into your house to shoot you dead in your sleep, it is important to avoid over-carbonation. As Hank found out, the sound of the bottle caps suddenly giving way to the immense gaseous pressure building up inside the bottles is a lot louder than you would think, and sounds remarkably like a gunshot.

todd alquist

Todd is almost the definition of a crazy fucking psychopath. He kills without fear or compunction, and has no problem with gunning down innocent women and children in cold-blood. And yet, weirdly, there is something almost likeable about him...

Despite his hardened criminal attitude, there is something child-like and innocent in his eagerness to please and his respect and loyalty towards those he sees as his betters that makes you always want to see the good in him. Until he takes out his gun and wastes someone else at a moment's notice.

He only had one season to make his mark, but it was one hell of a mark. Interestingly, when Walter meets him and begins to replace Jesse with him, Walter turns even more to the dark side. If we thought he was bad enough by the end, imagine what he would have been like if he had met Todd earlier?

NICKNAME: Ricky Hitler
OCCUPATION: Fumigator at Vamonos Pest Control; meth cook
FAVOURITE FOOD: The Work Lunch
BEST QUOTES:
Todd to Jesse, about shooting Drew Sharp: 'Man, shit happens, huh?'
Todd to his uncle: 'It was perfect. No one even knew they got robbed, just like we planned. Mr White told me it was, like, the biggest train heist ever, like, potential money-wise. So that's how that happened.'

conversion chart for weights and measures

DRY WEIGHT MEASUREMENTS

METRIC (GRAMS)	IMPERIAL (ounces and pounds)	US (cups and spoons)	
5 g	⅛ oz		
10 g	¼ oz		
15 g	½ oz	3 teaspoons	1 tablespoon
20 g	¾ oz		
30 g	1 oz	⅛ cup	2 tablespoons
40 g	1 ½ oz		
55 g	2 oz	¼ cup	4 tablespoons
65 g	2 ½ oz		
75 g	3 oz		
90 g	3 ½ oz		
105 g	4 oz (¼ lb)	½ cup	8 tablespoons
120 g	4 ½ oz		
135 g	4 ¾ oz		
150 g	5 oz		
165 g	5 ½ oz		
175 g	6 oz	¾ cup	12 tablespoons
185 g	6 ½ oz		
200 g	7 oz		
215 g	7 ½ oz		
225 g	8 oz (½ lb)	1 cup	16 tablespoons
250 g	9 oz		
275 g	10 oz		
300 g	11 oz		
450 g	16 oz (1 lb)	2 cups	32 tablespoons
500 g	18 oz		
1 kg	36 oz		

LIQUID OR VOLUME MEASUREMENTS

METRIC (millilitres)	FLUID OUNCES	BRITISH IMPERIAL	US
5 ml		1 teaspoon	1 teaspoon
15 ml	½ fl oz	1 tablespoon	1 tablespoon
20 ml	¾ fl oz		
30 ml	1 fl oz	2 tablespoons	2 tablespoons
40 ml	1 ½ fl oz		
60 ml	2 fl oz	4 tablespoons	¼ cup
85 ml	3 fl oz		
120 ml	4 fl oz		½ cup
150 ml	5 fl oz	¼ pint	
175 ml	6 fl oz		¾ cup
240 ml	8 fl oz		1 cup
300 ml	10 fl oz	½ pint	1 ¼ cup
350 ml	12 fl oz		
450 ml	15 fl oz	¾ pint	
475 ml	16 fl oz		2 cups
550 ml	18 fl oz		2 ¼ cups
600 ml	20 fl oz	1 pint	2 ½ cups
900 ml	30 fl oz	1 ½ pints	
1.2 litres	40 fl oz	2 pints	5 cups

OVEN TEMPERATURES

CELSIUS	FAHRENHEIT	GAS MARK
110	225	¼
120	250	½
140	275	1
150	300	2
160	325	3
180	350	4
190	375	5
200	400	6
220	425	7
230	450	8
240	475	9

CONVERSIONS FOR SPECIFIC INGREDIENTS

INGREDIENT	METRIC	IMPERIAL	US
All-purpose (plain) flour	150 g	5 oz	1 cup
Butter	110 g	4 oz	1 stick
	225 g	8 oz	1 cup
Caster sugar	225 g	8 oz	1 cup
Cocoa powder	115 g		1 cup
Double (heavy) cream		8 oz	1 cup
Golden syrup	350 g	12 oz	1 cup
Icing (powdered) sugar	110 g	4 oz	1 cup
Olive oil	15 ml	½ fl oz	1 tablespoon

index

Make your own. I've done enough.
Or you could use these pages to write
your own recipes and suggestions.
Suit yourself.